A
NAME
I
CAN'T
READ

The Rocky Road to Literacy: A Mother's Story

A NAME I CAN'T READ

The Rocky Road to Literacy: A Mother's Story

CLAUDIA M. DARKINS

CANE PUBLISHING
Houston, Texas

ISBN: 0-9648154-0-0

Subject Heading:Literacy//Ethnic Studies//African American
Studies//Education//Biography
Library of Congress Card Catalog Number: 97-92290
Printed in the United States of America

Darkins, Claudia M.
A Name I Can't Read: The Rocky Road to Literacy, A Mother's
Story

Edited by Marguerite Louise Butler and Brenda Willis

CANE PUBLISHING
P.O. Box 710544, Houston, TX. 77271-0544
Phone (713)541-5258 or (888)599-2263 Fax (713)541-5256

And so we arrived in enemy territory and they set me down at the enemy's door.

James Baldwin, <u>The Fire Next Time</u>

ACKNOWLEDGMENTS

A special thanks to my sons Gregory and Chris. Chris read part of the first draft of this book and told me that I needed to use the active voice and add emotion. He said that I wrote as if I stood outside a window looking in as the events unfolded. He reminded me that I was there and was a part of what happened. I told him that I just wanted to relate the facts. To this he replied, "Well Mom, feelings are facts and you need to drag them out and write them down." I protested that I was not sure I could do that. He persisted, "Mom, you can do it; let me show you an example of where you did it." He directed me to a passage that conveyed feelings. I started the arduous task of revising and became overwhelmed by the depth of my feelings and how grueling it was to write them down. I shuddered, cringed, gnawed my teeth, put the manuscript down and did not pick it up again for over three months.

Thanks to Gregory for showing his emotions. Upon hearing parts of this manuscript, Gregory turned away because remembering is still painful. This is a testimony to the statement that feelings are facts and should be woven into the fabric of this book.

An extra special thanks goes to Marguerite Louise Butler for her tireless effort over many months to take the milk toast out of this work and add a sense of urgency for those who read and may encounter what we have suffered and are still struggling to recover from.

Thanks to many friends who took the time to read this manuscript and offer words of advice and encouragement: Ron Thomas, Linda Clay, Iva Thomas, Jeffery Thomas, Etta Smith, Lisa Harris, Vicky Williams, Ralph Johnson, Virgie Faulk, Liz Nealy, Odell and Dorothy Davis. Thanks to Joe Samuel Ratliff, Elaine Mitchell, Jerome Thomas, Cheryl Bowmen, Clortis Roberts, Gloria Smith, Anthony Douglas and countless others who played a part leading to my finishing this work. A special thanks for the encouragement to Linda Garner who greeted me with the words "Hello, Sister Author" each time we met inside and outside the walls of Brentwood Baptist Church.

Thanks to my family. Thanks to my Mom, Hattie Hutton Jones, who reared thirteen children and showed me the heart of a mother. Thanks to Tonya for keeping me in mind while surfing the internet.

January, 1998   Claudia M. Darkins
Houston, Texas

Many of the names and places have been changed to protect the unwary victims, the guilty and the unassuming bystanders.

Contents

Acknowledgments

Introduction

1 The Beginning   15

2 Rude Awakening   19

3 The Truth Revealed   37

4 Waiting for a Change   51

5 A Cry for Help   61

6 Rays of Hope   97

7 The Cycle Continues   103

8 Low Expectations   119

9 Gregory at the Crossroads   139

10 Gregory, Nowhere to Hide   143

11 Avoiding the Pitfalls   149

12 Contrasts and Comparisons   157

13 Current Day Case Studies   171

14 Where Do We Go From Here   183

Epilogue   191

Author's Note   193

Glossary   194

Bibliography   195

Index   196

INTRODUCTION

Undoubtedly, some of you will read the title of this book, perhaps even the introduction and believe that its content does not
pertain to you. I wish you were right, but **I would not be willing
to stake my child's future on it**. I urge you to read on, become
aware and you will be better equipped to help ebb the high tide of
illiteracy in our homes, our communities and our nation.

Illiteracy has reached epidemic proportions among young
Americans. On a daily basis, we encounter a large number of in-
telligent, youth who are functionally illiterate. Many of these children are the offspring of middle and working class parents who
often are college educated. Some of these children are in school,
others have graduated; many have dropped out of school and do
what they can to survive. The impact of illiteracy is devastating for
all concerned: the children, the parents, the community, our nation.

Do you wonder why we have such a staggering illiteracy
problem in this country where, theoretically, provisions have been
made to educate all of our children? I have searched for reasons
for this phenomena from my experiences and I can tell you what I
have found to be a major contributing factor to illiteracy among
minorities in America. This contributing factor, simply stated, is
the willful exclusion of children from the teaching/learning process during the primary grades. In this book, I show you how
exclusion is accomplished. I relate the educational experiences of
my children spanning from the 1970's through the 1990's. After

that, I present case studies to show that what happened to my children is not peculiar to them. Following that, I provide valuable insight concerning what we can do to combat illiteracy.

Once you've read this book and understand the intricacies of the information within, you will be aware of what is happening to the academic foundation of too many of our children. Often, our children are robbed of the opportunity to gain a meaningful education before they can understand what is happening to them. Through no fault of their own, they fall behind and their futures become replete with inexplicable academic hurdles. Parents usually do not understand the dilemma and may allow the blame to fall on the child or themselves.

By reading this book you will become aware of one of the major causes of illiteracy and you will be given strategies for combating illiteracy among your children and the children in your community.

I
The Beginning

Not so long ago, in 1971 and 1974, two Black boys were born in the United States of America. Who would not take it for granted that they would go to school and be taught to read, write and be counted? My Family took it for granted and we were in for a rude awakening.

Gregory

Gregory, my first child, was born in San Francisco, California in 1971. He was delivered by natural childbirth. Gregory weighed 6 pounds 14 ounces and measured 21.5 inches in length.

Gregory was born with a head full of natural hair (an afro); I was not able to smooth it with my hand and a little oil as my mother had done for her babies during their first weeks of life. Gregory's "natural" made me smile and I fondly tell about it at family gatherings and in pleasant company, even today.

As soon as Gregory and I arrived home from the hospital, I started reading to him, telling him stories, playing with him and just talking to him in general. As a young mother, I spent a lot of time nurturing Gregory. I took every opportunity to turn daily activities into learning experiences for him. Gregory counted ducks at the pond, counted cars by color as we went on daily excursions, and I read to him most every night. When he awoke hungry or needing a diaper change, I took him into the family room to rock and sing to him.

I bought books for Gregory before he was born and continued to buy books and other learning materials for him as time went on. As a child, Gregory had a wonderful disposition. He enjoyed the time we shared and the learning activities we did together. Gregory learned to recite and write all 26 letters of the alphabet, count to 20 and developed a wonderful way with colors before he was old enough to enter Kindergarten. Gregory liked playing with building blocks, Lincoln logs, toy trains and race cars.

My maternity leave ran out when Gregory was six weeks old and I went back to work at the Department of Social Services. Gregory's first babysitters were some of our friends who cared for him in their homes. His last babysitter in San Francisco was Mrs. Wash. Gregory stayed with Mrs. Wash until his brother, Chris, was born. After that Gregory went to a church school day care located on the lower end of Market street. In the church day care, Gregory was described as being quiet and easy going. Gregory stayed in that day care until we moved to Illinois in February 1975.

Christopher

Christopher, my second child, was born in San Francisco, California, in 1974. Delivered by natural childbirth, 30 days after his scheduled due date, Chris weighed 7 pounds 9 ounces and measured 20 inches in length.

When Chris was about ten weeks old, I went back to work. My youngest sister babysat both Gregory and Chris until she returned home at the end of Summer to finish high school. After that, we took Chris to Mrs. Wash for child care while Gregory went to a church day care.

During his early years, Chris exhibited a very easy going personality and did not fuss a lot. Like his older brother, Chris enjoyed playing with building blocks, Lincoln logs, toy cars, trucks and trains. He played well by himself and with his older brother. He especially liked for me to play with them. Once, while doing a Mother's Day project at his day care, Chris responded to the question "What are mothers for?" by saying: "To play, to make a heart, nothing else." His response was written on a poster and I cried when I received it. His words really touched my heart.

Chris liked being helpful and offered to help whenever he saw me doing things around the house. He amazed me with how easily he understood directions and accomplished tasks not normally expected of a child so young.

Chris, an obedient child, took pride in doing as he was told. I did not have to worry about him wandering off and getting lost because he stayed close at hand. I always felt that I could reach out and touch him. He did not go to the homes of his friends without asking first, and when he was told "no", he obeyed. Chris was also a grateful child. He appreciated anything that you gave him or did for him. He genuinely said thank you for gifts given to him, whether they were new or hand-me-downs. Chris was very observant as a child. By watching his older brother, he potty trained himself by the time he turned one year old.

Chris eagerly sought to learn new things. For instance, shortly after Gregory started taking swimming lessons, Chris wanted to take lessons too. However, his brother was taking lessons at the YMCA and they did not offer classes for children as young as Chris. Chris persisted in his complaint that he would not be able to swim because I didn't enroll him in class. Eventually, I enrolled both Chris and Gregory in class at the YWCA. Chris wanted to learn to swim and become good at it, so he worked hard and did very well. When Chris became old enough, I switched them both back to the YMCA and they continued to do well in their swim lessons.

2

Rude Awakening

When Gregory reached 3 ½ years old and Chris was 10 months old, our family moved from California to Illinois. My husband's company transferred him to Elk Grove Village and we settled nearby in a large apartment complex in Mt. Prospect. The area where we moved was booming with new businesses and jobs were plentiful at the time.

We did not know anyone in the immediate area, so my husband and I agreed that I would not work until our youngest child, Chris, could attend day care. At that time, most day care facilities did not take children until they were 2 years old and potty trained.

Our family quickly settled into our new community. We joined the YMCA in Des Plaines, a city near Mt. Prospect, which boasted having the largest YMCA in the USA at that time. Gregory and Chris took swimming and gymnastic lessons at the "Y". The boys and I frequented the library and public parks. We also enjoyed the playground and recreation area provided for residents of the apartment complex where we lived.

I became the AVON representative serving our apartment complex. Sometimes, when I delivered sales books, the boys accompanied me riding on their tricycle or big wheel. At other times, I left them with my downstairs neighbor, Judy, who had two young children. Judy had a daughter, Jenny, who was a year or so older than Gregory, and a son Michael, who was about the same age as Gregory. The children played well together and enjoyed the time they spent together. As the AVON representative, I became familiar with many of the residents that I might not otherwise have become acquainted with. We also got to know each others children which meant that the boys were recognized by a lot of children and had many playmates. Gregory, a very outgoing child, made friends easily with children throughout the apartment complex. He had plenty of time to play with his friends because he did not have to leave home for day care.

Gregory in Kindergarten

In September, 1976, after having lived in Mt. Prospect for about a year and a half, Gregory reached Kindergarten age. We enrolled him at Live Oak Elementary School. Live Oak Elementary, a fairly new school, was situated just off the grounds of the apartment complex where we lived.

After enrollment, Gregory and I attended Kindergarten orientation. We gathered in one of the Kindergarten classrooms along with the rest of the parents and children. The teachers explained the skills the children were expected to know when they started and the skills they were expected to learn in kindergarten.

I did not worry about Gregory doing well in school. He already knew the skills the teachers expected children to know. Also, he knew most of the skills the teachers said would be taught in Kindergarten. At home: Gregory used scissors and glue for cutting and pasting; he wrote, recited and recognized the 26 letters of the alphabet; he counted to 20 and knew the basic colors. Also, he had completed a number of math and reading workbooks for preschoolers. I went away from the orientation feeling very confident that Gregory would do well in school.

Prior to school starting, a parent's meeting was held to report good news about a large grant the school would receive from the federal government. The community was experiencing tremendous economic growth, and there was an influx of people from diverse ethnic and cultural backgrounds. This influx of diverse people was the basis for the funding request and the amount received was tremendous.

At this same meeting, parents were urged to sign up as volunteers for various school activities and functions. I volunteered to work in the library during the half day that Gregory attended his Kindergarten class.

The school was across the playground from our apartment complex and the children did not have to cross any major streets to get there. After the first few days of school, Gregory and a few of his classmates began walking to school without any parents accompanying them. About thirty minutes after Gregory left for school, Chris and I walked to the school for me to do my volunteer work in the library.

While I worked in the library, Chris looked through books and played with the things we brought from home to occupy his time. Chris also enjoyed listening when Gregory's class came in the library for story time. I checked books out to the children and became acquainted with them all. Mrs. Saturn, Gregory's teacher, usually complimented me on my work in the library. She told me how well behaved Gregory was and how much she enjoyed having him in her class.

A few weeks after school started, my downstairs neighbor asked me to stop by because she wanted to talk to me about something she had noticed. She usually saw Gregory when he came home from school because she lived downstairs and kept a keen eye out for both our children. Her son, also in Kindergarten, did not attend school during the same half day session as Gregory. However, she noticed that Gregory did not bring home any of the awards that her son brought home from school and she wondered why.

She showed the awards to me: a large thick cardboard lace up shoe given to children who could tie their own shoes; a play telephone given to children who knew their phone number;

a house given to children who knew their home address. She wanted to know why Gregory had not brought any of these awards home because she knew that he could tie his shoes, say and dial his phone number and recite his address. I told her that Gregory's teacher had never mentioned giving out the awards, but that I would ask her about them when I went to school for open house.

At the open house, Gregory's teacher made it a point to compliment me on my work in the library. I took this as an opportunity to ask her if Gregory was having a problem in class with tying his shoes, saying his address or phone number. She said he was not having any problems. I told her that I asked because Gregory did not bring home any of the awards given to the children in the other kindergarten class for showing that they knew or could do those things. She said she would check on the awards. At the end of the next school day, Gregory came home with all of the awards at the same time. I vaguely remember thinking that it seemed odd for him to get all of the awards on the same day.

When it was time for progress reports, I made an appointment for a conference with Mrs. Saturn. When I went in, she had a completed checklist indicating that Gregory had mastered the skills specified on the checklist. Mrs. Saturn gave Gregory a very good progress report with the exception that she said he had one letter of the alphabet out of place. I later discovered that this problem stemmed from Gregory's failure to understand Mrs. Saturn's speech pattern. When she said the letter, it sounded like another letter to him. When he tried to imitate her, he said what the letter sounded like when she said it. (The text of the progress report follows on the next pages.)

Also, during the first months of the school year, I noticed something unusual at home. As I served meals, Gregory would say, "Mommy, please don't give me my milk last." I wondered if I unknowingly showed favoritism toward Gregory's younger brother. I started being mindful of this in an effort to minimize the likelihood of my showing favoritism.

COMMUNITY CONSOLIDATED SCHOOL DISTRICT 59
Elk Grove Township, Illinois

KINDERGARTEN CONFERENCE SUMMARY SHEET (Revised 1971)

To be filled out before Parent Conference; insert in Cumulative Folder

CHILD'S NAME _Greg Dorkin_

DATE OF APPOINTMENT _Dec 3 1976_ TEACHER _Holly Saturn_

PARENT PRESENT FOR APPOINTMENT _Mother_

Many activities are planned to help the child develop mentally, socially, physically, emotionally and culturally by learning to do the following things:

Your child	Usually	At Times	Seldom
Listens when other speak	✓		
Follows directions	✓		
Takes turns - plays well with others	needs to work on		
Speaks in complete sentences		✓	
Speaks before a group easily		✓	
Participates in group conversations		✓	
Shows ability to discuss stories	✓		
Is able to put thoughts into words easily		✓	
Stays on subject when talking	✓		
Accepts responsibility for his actions	✓		
Can assemble simple puzzles	✓		
Recognizes squares, circles, triangles, ellipsis and rectangles			
Is able to copy a simple pattern on paper		✓	
Knows whole name, address and phone number	✓		
Is able to tie, button and zip	✓		
Can interpret pictures	✓		
Sees likenesses and differences in objects and pictures	✓		
Is able to count and make simple sets	✓		

23

A Name I Can't Read

KINDERGARTEN COMPETENCE SHEET — PAGE 2

	Usually	At Times	Seldom
Recognizes and uses colors	✓	—	—
Expresses himself creatively through the use of rhythms, dramatizations, songs and speech	*tends to be shy*	—	—
Responds to music activities	✓	—	—
Shows curiosity and interest in things around him	✓	—	—
Shows large muscle skills as needed to skip, hop, and walk a balance beam easily	—	✓	—
Shows ability in uses of pencils, scissors, and crayons	—	*His small muscle coordination is developing*	—
Can repeat simple clapping patterns	—	—	—
Is courteous to others	✓	—	—

SUMMARY

Tony tends to be a shy but very bright student with an excellent vocabulary and a good ability to listen to directions carefully. He is shy when he acts out stories and is hesitant to share his ideas with the class. He is very ready for kindergarten and enjoys all types of activities. His small muscle could use time for development to make art activities more enjoyable.

24

The Christmas Party

As the Christmas holidays approached, we received a notice from school about the Christmas party. The notice explained that there would not be a Christmas party for the children unless enough parents volunteered to help with the planning and preparation. I volunteered to help with telephone calls to parents before the party and to help in the classroom on the day of the party.

Before the party, we called parents to find out the name of a toy they had already purchased their child for Christmas. We gave the list of items to the teacher. Then, on the day of the party, when the teacher took a child across the room to see Santa, she was to tell Santa the name of the item the parent(s) had already bought. Santa would then promise that item to the child for Christmas.

On the day of the party, we gathered in the classroom. Tables were set up for the children to sit and enjoy their goodies. I worked at a table other than the one where Gregory sat.

During the party, volunteers took the children's holiday papers down from the wall and gave them to Mrs. Saturn for her to pass out. Mrs. Saturn called the children by name as she passed the papers out. Along the way, she said, "A name I can't read", and moved that paper to the bottom of the stack. At the end, she called Gregory's name and gave him his paper. She had only one paper left in her hand. She did the same thing with another set of papers as she passed them out.

Since I volunteered in the library and was acquainted with the children; I knew that one little girl was absent. I realized that there were no names that Mrs. Saturn could not read. She had given Gregory his papers last on purpose. I began to critically observe her actions.

Eventually, the time arrived for the children to see Santa. Mrs. Saturn called the children one by one and took them over to see Santa. She whispered into Santa's ear the name of the item the parent(s) had bought for the child. When she had called the name of almost every child in the room, Gregory got up from where he sat and came over to where I stood. He put his arms around my left leg and laid his head against me. After Mrs. Saturn called all of the other children to see Santa, she turned and looked towards where we stood.

"Why Greg, you mean you haven't seen Santa yet.", she said. In a calm voice, I said, "Mrs. Saturn, you've called every other child in here, but you haven't called Gregory to see Santa yet."

Mrs. Saturn, standing in the middle of the floor, stretched out her hand and Gregory walked over to her. She took a side step with Gregory, and then, with a slight shove of the hand, motioned him to go on over to see Santa by himself. She did not whisper into Santa's ear the name of the item we bought for Santa to promise him.

After a moment, while still standing in the middle of the floor, Mrs. Saturn turned to us raising her hands with exuberance.

"And now, for the younger sisters and brothers!", she exclaimed.

As she spoke, she turned and moved across the room away from us. She started talking to a father who sat with his son on his lap. Both father and son were blond haired and looked very wholesome. By this time, Gregory had returned to stand beside me.

"Do you think that your little brother would like to see Santa?", I said to Gregory.

"Oh yes!", he said beaming.

Immediately, Gregory took Chris by the hand and lead him over to see Santa. Santa picked Chris up onto his lap and reached into the box picking up the last bag. As if by instinct, Mrs. Saturn turned from the man and boy. She literally ran across the room and snatched the bag from Santa's hand.

"Someone hasn't seen Santa yet!", she exclaimed, waving the bag in her hand.

Rude Awakening

Santa convinced her that he needed something from the bag to give the child on his lap. I looked on in horror for what Gregory must have suffered these months since school started in September.

As the party came to an end, Mrs. Saturn came over to offer me the usual compliments for the work that I do as a volunteer. I held on to Chris' hand and just looked at her piercingly. I felt heartsick and enraged. My urge was to take hold and just shake her. Instead, I stood firm with my body tense and my jaws tight. When Gregory finished bundling up, I took his hand in my other and we left. This was the last day of school before the Christmas holidays.

Over the holidays, I mulled over what I had seen that day at the Christmas party. I realized why Gregory did not want to be given his milk last. I remembered the awards that I had to ask about before he received them. I realized that he would not have received the awards at all if my neighbor had not known about them, wondered why Gregory had not received them, and mentioned it to me.

When the holidays were over, Gregory went off to school as he normally did. He went to Mrs. Saturn's class as always. I, on the other hand, went to talk to Mrs. Gillory, the Principal at Live Oak Elementary. I could not think of any reason to talk to Mrs. Saturn after what I had seen on the day of the Christmas party. As soon as I got to the principal's office, I let her know there was a problem.

I told her about the Christmas party - the "name I can't read" and the visit with Santa. I told her about the manifestation of the problem that I saw at home. I told her about Gregory not wanting to get his milk last. I even told her how I had to inquire about the awards given for knowing how to tie your shoes, remember your phone number and address before she gave them to Gregory all on the same day. I interjected that the pride and sense of accomplishment that Gregory should have felt by receiving such awards must have been lost in the process of having them dumped on him unceremoniously.

I told Mrs. Gillory that I did not want Gregory to remain in Mrs. Saturn's class because nothing she might teach him could possibly be worth the damage she was inflicting on his self-esteem. I wanted Gregory removed from Mrs. Saturn's class as soon as possible.

Mrs. Gillory seemed to listen intently as I told her why I wanted Gregory moved out of Mrs. Saturn's class.

After I finished, she said, "You do know that Gregory is being removed from the classroom every morning for about 15 minutes?"

"What?", I said shocked. "What are you saying?" "Why is he being removed from the classroom?" (I usually arrived at school within an hour after school started, and he was in the classroom whenever I happened to look in.)

"Well", she told me, "we can't officially remove Kindergarten children from the classroom for special help. Mrs. Saturn should have gotten your agreement before referring him for special help.", she continued matter-of-fact.

I asked Mrs. Gillory what special help he was being referred for. She said she preferred to have the special teacher who worked with Gregory come in and explain why he was sent to her.

I waited while the principal went to let the special teacher know I wanted to talk with her. When the special teacher arrived, the three of us continued our conference in the principal's office.

The special teacher said Mrs. Saturn referred Gregory to her because he did not know his letters, his numbers or his colors. She sent for him during the first fifteen minutes of class so that he would miss socialization time and would not miss any other class work time.

For the children referred to her, she worked with only a few letters of the alphabet (I cannot remember how many she mentioned, although I think it was five.). She worked with up to eight numbers and the five basic colors. I told them I was truly surprised about all this because Gregory did not have to come to this school to learn his letters, his numbers or his colors. He knew those things well before he started school. Also, I was surprised because, during our conference, Mrs. Saturn had given me a signed progress report indicating that Gregory knew his letters, numbers and colors. During the conference, she did not indicate that he had problems or needed special help.

I asked the special teacher why she didn't know that Gregory knew these things. If she worked with Gregory every day, she should have found out what he knows long before now. She said Gregory did nothing for her when she sent for him.

"Do you ask him to do anything?", I asked amazed not expecting anything more than the nod that she gave in response.

I wasn't sure what to think about her saying he did nothing for her. I directed the conversation back to the point of Gregory's removal from the class and told them it had been a long time since I had been in grade school, but socialization time was the time that I remember enjoying more than any other time. I related that I fondly remember the songs and the "get to know you" activities we did each morning in school. However, the memory of learning to read, write and count is rather vague. I suggested that removing a child from class during socialization time bordered on cruelty. (Another thought that I later had was that this might explain why Gregory did not receive the awards for knowing how to tie his shoes, or recite his address and phone number. Socialization time might be the time when they did that activity.)

I asked the special teacher to show me where she took Gregory when he was sent to her. She directed me to a small inner room off from the library. The special teacher showed me a box with some color crayons and a few other items she used with the children referred to her. I was not impressed, but felt depressed at the idea that Gregory was brought to this little room each morning to have a box with a few letters and some crayon in it presented to him. Whatever the intent, it must have been a mystery to Gregory since, according to the special teacher, he did nothing with it.

We returned to the principal's office. I told them that I still did not fully understand why the special teacher had a problem determining that Gregory did not need special help with recognizing his letters, numbers and colors. As far as why he did nothing for her, maybe the small room and the lack of challenging work prevented him from responding. Maybe the timing of when he was removed from the classroom impacted him. In any case, I asked that the special teacher have Gregory write his alphabets from A to Z and his numbers from 1 to 20. I told her to give him a blank sheet of paper with no reference, and to tell him that she wanted him to write his letters from A to Z and his numbers from 1 to 20 on the paper. I also requested that she not take him into the small room, but to use a table in the library or some other open area. I was very sure of Gregory's ability to do this and told them that I did not have to watch when the special teacher told him to do this. I would come back to see the results.

When I returned to the principal's office the next school day, Mrs. Gillory had a large piece of construction paper. On that sheet of construction paper, Gregory had written the letters of the alphabet and numbers from 1 to 20. He had done a very good job. The number 5 was turned the wrong way, but all the numbers and letters were very well formed and legible. Gregory had accomplished the task without any instructions other than a statement of what to do.

The Principal told me that she had talked to Mrs. Saturn about what happened and that Mrs. Saturn was very sorry about the error. She asked me if I would agree to meet with Mrs. Saturn and consider leaving Gregory in the class with her. I explained to Mrs. Gillory that after seeing Mrs. Saturn in action at the Christmas party, I felt uncomfortable having Gregory in her classroom. Also, I simply would not trust anything she had to say to me even if we met. Therefore, I did not want to meet with her.

Rude Awakening

Before Gregory switched class sessions, Mrs. Saturn approached me in the library. She said that she would hate very much for Gregory to leave her class. I could not imagine what she expected me to say. I just looked at her and grunted, "uh huh."

When Gregory changed his class session, I, accordingly, changed the time I worked in the library. Gregory's new class came to the library just as his previous class had. Usually, when they came in, the teacher held Michael, my downstairs neighbor's son, by the hand. Michael, no bigger than your average 3 year old, and Gregory were the best of friends. (In the statement written by Mrs. Seville regarding Gregory, Michael is probably the child referred to when she indicates that Gregory developed a close friendship with one little boy and got along extremely well with him. Gregory and Michael were already friends.)

I volunteered in the library for another couple of months until I returned to work. I notified the school that I planned to start back to work and asked that they keep me informed about Gregory's progress although I would no longer be volunteering in the library.

Because I would no longer be at home when his school day began or ended, we enrolled Gregory and Chris in the Children's World Day Care Center in Mt. Prospect. I took them there in the mornings before I went to work and the children's center took Gregory to school and picked him up from school for after school care.

As far as I could tell, the rest of Gregory's kindergarten year went smoothly. At least, his new teacher did not notify me that there were any problems. However, over 4 years later, when Gregory went to the Brentwood Christian Academy, a report from Live Oak Elementary surfaced. It was written by Mrs. Seville, the new kindergarten teacher that Gregory was assigned to after he had left Mrs. Saturn's class. Miss Seville did not discuss or show the report to us at the time. However, it appears that she was attempting to establish some type of profile on Gregory. My impression of Miss Seville was that she was very young, new to the teaching profession and did not have the experience or training necessary to do specialized profiles on children. Yet this report went into Gregory's school file and followed him from school to school. We heard about it when the administration at Brentwood Christian Academy inquired about the reason for the report. We asked for a copy of the report, and it appears on the next page.

COMMUNITY CONSOLIDATED SCHOOL DISTRICT 59

ELK GROVE TOWNSHIP SCHOOLS
BOARD OF EDUCATION AND ADMINISTRATIVE OFFICES

2123 S. Arlington Heights Road · Arlington Heights, Illinois 60005 · Phone 312/593-4300

Superintendent
Roger Barnwell

Re: Greg Darkins

From: Debbie Seville

Greg came in to my class in mid-year seemingly having a low self-concept.
Since that time he has developed a more positive self-image but there are
many things I feel are still puzzling about Greg.

Greg was welcomed to our class with open arms but seems to be either a
withdrawn child or a very selective one -- taking much care in selecting
his friends. He developed a close friendship with one little boy and got
along extremely well with him. He did not interact with the other children
very easily; he seemed to enjoy observing them instead.

Greg appears to be confused when given oral directions but when working
with him on a one-to-one basis he seems to have the ability - such as
distinguishing between beginning sounds associating certain sounds to
given letters, explaining certain concepts verbally, joining sets, making
comparisons of sets, etc.

As Greg's teacher, one needs to be aware of his special needs and keep
a watchful eye on him or he may get lost in the crowd. He is a very quiet,
maybe somewhat introverted child, and needs to be drawn out.

June 1977

Gregory in First Grade

There were very few black families in the apartment complex with children Gregory's age. However, one Black couple had a 10 year old son named Mark. I asked his parents how things were for him at Live Oak Elementary. His mother said they were going back and forth with members of the school's staff trying to solve a problem they were having with the school. They discovered that Mark scored at genius level on the Math and Science portion of one of the standardized test that he was given at the school. However, the school did not place Mark in the Accelerated Math and Science program that was available. Instead, the school had Mark helping other children with their work during his class time. Mark's mother expressed that they were very frustrated about the situation.

Gregory continued at Live Oak Elementary for First Grade. His teacher, Mrs. Canada, said that Gregory did well in her class and that his skills gained him placement in next to the top reading group. She also explained that she watched Gregory on the playground because she wondered how the other children treated him since he is Black and the other children are White. She reported that he got along well with the other children and had a lot of friends in the class.

We explained to her that she did not have to worry about that because Gregory lived in the same apartment complex with many of the children in the class, and they played at each other's homes and out of doors together without apparent problems.

Mrs. Canada mentioned that Gregory did not respond quickly when she called upon him in class. She said he seemed to think before speaking and gave the impression of being fearful that his answer would not be correct. However, she said his answers were usually right. I told her that his not responding quickly might be a trait he inherited from my father. My father was slow to answer questions. He thought before answering questions and seemingly considered the possibilities of the question.

Rude Awakening

Gregory's dad chuckled and said, "In other words, he is deliberate and there's nothing to worry about."

We left it at that and we felt comfortable with Gregory being in Mrs. Canada's class that last year at Live Oak Elementary. However, years later after we moved to Texas, I asked to see Gregory's school record. It contained a form that had an obvious reference to that conversation, but the light in which Mrs. Canada presented the conversation is questionable. It implies that Gregory is "slow" rather than that he is slow to answer questions (see below).

✓ Live Oak	School
	Teacher
	Level
	Age

Child's Name

Instructions: The Anecdotal Growth Record should refer to evaluated by teacher's judgement. State a specific inc... ord test scores on this report or use such terms as "go... permanent record folder for further explanation.

Greg is a very slow-worker who wants to be sure he is right. His father says he is "deliberate." He needs constant assurance. He is well liked by his peer group and likes to play.

Social & Emotional Growth – including attitude toward peers and adults

Attitudes taste in r... ing & libr... program

ANECDOTAL GRO

35

A Name I Can't Read

Chris in Day Care

Chris was happy when we enrolled him in the Children's World Day Care Center. He associated going to day care with learning and he was excited. Chris really wanted to be taught to read. One day a class leader advised me that Chris did not participate in some of the optional activities. She said he usually sat in a corner of the room while the optional activities were taking place.

When I talked to Chris about this, he said that the teacher said the activities were optional and that he didn't have to do them.

"Well, why don't you do them anyway?", I suggested.

He responded, "I want to learn to read, so I look through books while they are playing."

I noticed that there were bookshelves full of children's books in the corner where the teacher said Chris sat during the optional activities. I related what Chris told me to the class leader.

Chris continued in the regular day care program until he became old enough for the Montessori class they offered. The Montessori class included formal learning activities in conjunction with the day care. Chris was glad to get into the Montessori class because he thought he would be taught to read.

However, Chris did not like being the first person to arrive at school for the Montessori program. We turned the lights on, put his things away and then he went to the classroom next door. One of the administrators explained that most of the children in the Montessori class came to the children's center just for that class. The class did not start until later in the day, so no one was in the Montessori classroom when we arrived. Chris remained in the Montessori class at Children's World until he and his brother left the center after Gregory finished First Grade.

3
The Truth Revealed

We started looking for a single family home during Gregory's First Grade year at Live Oak Elementary. We decided on a home in a new housing development on the East side of Elgin. By the middle of the school year our house was finished, and we moved to the Oakwood subdivision. Gregory and Chris continued attending the Children's World Day Care Center in Mt. Prospect for day care and the day care center continued to take Gregory to school and pick him up for after school care.

Although we planned for the children to stay at the Children's World Day Care Center until school ended, we began searching for child care in Elgin so that we would have that settled by summer. We found a babysitter in the subdivision where we lived; and she lived on our street. She had a son the same age as Gregory and younger twin daughters. As soon as Gregory finished First Grade at Live Oak Elementary, he started going to this neighbor's home for child care, and he continued going there once school started in the fall. We enrolled Chris for day care at Young's Corner in Elgin.

Gregory in Second Grade

In Elgin, we enrolled Gregory in Second Grade at the neighborhood school. Wren's Lake Elementary was a relatively new school located near the clubhouse and set just off the grounds of the subdivision where we lived. The children could walk or ride their bikes across the playground to school within a few minutes.

The children and I visited the school before it started in order to get a feel for what it was like. It appeared to be a very nice, quiet school. We talked with the principal, and he made me feel very comfortable. The school used a different reading series from the one used at Live Oak Elementary. However, I did not think a change in Reading series would be a problem and did not worry about that. Yet, I felt anxious about the change in schools because of Gregory's bad experiences in Kindergarten at Live Oak Elementary.

After school had been in session for a short while, I started asking Gregory about his reading class in school. His response a number of times was that he did not have reading that day. I started questioning him closer by asking him to tell me the name of the book he read in school and by asking him to tell me about one of the stories he read. Looking apprehensive, Gregory told me that he did not have a reading book. At first, I felt sure he must mean something other than what he said, and my inclination was to regard his statement as being idle. Nevertheless, I agonized over my uneasiness and decided to check it out with Gregory's teacher.

I went to the school for a conference with Gregory's teacher. Mrs. Kieper was rather young, and I thought she probably had just started teaching. I inquired about Gregory's progress, and Mrs. Kieper said that he was doing well in his studies. I asked to see the reading book Gregory used in class, but Mrs. Kieper said they used several different books to keep the children from getting bored. She pointed out the shelves that held the different books that she said they used. She explained that policy prevented the teachers from letting the children take the books home. They did not want the children to read ahead and then not want to read the same thing again in class. At this point, I told her what Gregory had said about not having a reading book.

She grinned and said, "I assure you, Mrs. Darkins, he does have a reading book. You don't have to worry about that."

The Truth Revealed

After I got home, I talked to Gregory about my meeting with Mrs. Kieper. I asked him why he said he didn't have a reading book because Mrs. Kieper had shown me the different books they used for reading. Then, Gregory told me he didn't have a reading book because Mrs. Kieper said all the other children could read and because he could not, he could not be in a reading group. This disturbed me and I became even more disturbed when Gregory said that Mrs. Kieper told him that if he read, he would miss gym and not have any fun. I could not believe what I was hearing. I took one of the books off the shelf that Gregory finished reading while at Live Oak Elementary.

"You can read this book.", I told Gregory.

"No, I can't read!", he said and shrank away.

"Yes, you can read this book Gregory. You read it in first grade and you can still read it!"

Finally, Gregory started reading the book. He was very excited that he could still read the book.

He smiled and said, "I told Mrs. Kieper I could read, but she said, 'no.'" His excitement showed.

I felt drained and agitated. I asked Gregory what he did during reading time.

"I don't do anything, some women come and get me from class and take me to a room. They give me some paper, but they don't give me any work to do." His humiliation showed and I was dumbfounded. My heart ached and I became breathless.

Incensed, I went back to the school to talk to Mrs. Kieper. I asked her what time they met for reading. She said the time they read depended on what other things they had to do.

I told her that I asked because Gregory had again told me he didn't have a reading book and that she was not teaching him to read. I told her that he informed me that while she teaches reading to the other children, some women come get him and take him to a room to do nothing. I looked at her intensely. She said that what she does for Gregory is send him out for individual help from some of the special people they have at the school.

A Name I Can't Read

"Then, you don't have him in a reading group, and you're not teaching him to read?" I asked as my pulse raced involuntarily.

She looked at me, then she looked away and back again. She told me that most of the children in the class had been in reading groups together before, and she didn't want to put Gregory in with them without special help. It was then that I realized the truthfulness of Gregory's first statement that he did not have a reading book. There were many books on the shelves, but he was not being taught from any of them. I became angrier as the moments passed and I felt torn apart because of the unconscionable turmoil that Gregory's teacher subjected him to each day at this new school.

I asked Mrs. Kieper who the special people were and what materials they used to help Gregory. She replied that a group of mothers volunteered to provide special help for children who need it. They were called the "Super Moms". About the material they used, she did not know.

I asked her who was responsible for telling the "Super Moms" what Gregory needed help with and for giving them material to use. She said she didn't know the answer to that. I was very upset and had a difficult time controlling my emotions. I moved closer to Mrs. Kieper and in a stern, tense, yet controlled voice told her that she was trying to destroy my child; and make him appear stupid by keeping him out of the reading groups with the other children. She grimaced and shrugged slightly while making fleeting eye contact with me. She obviously did not care how I felt, but was made uncomfortable by my presence.

I walked out of Mrs. Kieper classroom and went directly to the principal's office. I informed Mr. Palmer that I had found out that my son was not being taught reading at Wren Lake School. Instead, Mrs. Kieper was having volunteer mothers take him out of the room while she taught reading to the other children and she did not give the volunteer mothers any material for working with Gregory.

The Truth Revealed

The Principal looked at me and did not comment on what I told him except to say that he could not respond until he talked to the teacher about this. He said he would check into the situation and call me.

A few days later, Mr. Palmer called and said he had talked to Mrs. Kieper. He said that it was a misunderstanding that the "Super Moms" were not given any materials to use for working with
Gregory. He said they were in the process of determining where Gregory should be placed in reading, but he would be placed.

Confused about what was happening to Gregory and afraid there might really be something that I needed to understand about my child and school, I called Live Oak Elementary and left a message for Mrs. Canada, Gregory's first grade teacher, to call me. I reasoned that she must have a logical explanation for what was happening to Gregory. Mrs. Canada returned my call. I told her who I was. She remembered. I asked her if there was anything about Gregory's reading that I should know. Did he have a problem of some sort? She responded that Gregory did very well in reading in her class and he liked participating.

I explained that I inquired because his teacher at Wren Lake Elementary was not teaching him to read with the other children. I told her that Gregory's new teacher sent him from the classroom during his reading period for special help from the "Super Moms". Mrs. Canada assured me that Gregory did well in her class, and she knew of no reason why he should not do well at Wren Lake Elementary.

About a week later, Gregory brought home a note from Mrs. Kieper. The note stated that he needed to improve his reading. I visited the school. I told Mrs. Kieper that Gregory had been reading at home and seemed to be doing fine. For that reason, I wanted to help him using the book he used in school. I asked her for a school book to use in order to assist him with his reading at home. She denied my request by saying the school did not have an extra book. She also explained that since she sent the note, she

41

had again started sending Gregory to the "Super Moms" for extra help. She said Gregory had improved in his reading, and he was now completing his assignments on time.

Later, when I questioned Gregory about his reading at school, he told me that one day he had gone to Mrs. Spears' class during reading time. He said that he was not reading in Mrs. Kieper's class because she said that all of her reading groups were full and he could not be in any one of them. (It sounded as if they were giving him excuses for not teaching him in his own class and the excuse was that there was no room in the groups for him - he was the odd child out.)

I had not heard of Mrs. Spears before, and I went to the school to find out what was happening with Gregory's placement in reading. The Principal told me that all the reading groups in Mrs. Kieper's room were full and the other children were too far along in the reading book to start another child. Therefore, he arranged to place Gregory in a small reading group with Mrs. Spears, one of the other Second Grade teachers. The Principal explained that they placed Gregory in a level 7 reading group and that level 7 should take about six weeks to complete. Gregory would go to Mrs. Spears just for reading and would continue to take all of his other classes in Mrs. Kieper's classroom. He requested that they be given several weeks to work with Gregory in his new group before I came back to the school for a conference regarding his progress. By this time November had arrived; we made plans to meet again in early December.

In early December, I returned to the school for the scheduled meeting with the principal, Mrs. Kieper, and Mrs. Spears. At the beginning of the meeting, Mrs. Kieper presented the results from two tests and said she gave them to Gregory at the beginning of the school year before deciding to put him with the "Super Moms" instead of in one of her regular reading groups. She explained that the first test concerned "what you should know after Level 6" and the second test concerned "what you should know after Level 7".

The Truth Revealed

Gregory scored 100% on the first test and 40% on the second test. She gave this as her reason for placing him with the "Super Moms" instead of with one of the reading groups. I asserted that the 100% score on the post Level 6 test clearly indicated that she should have placed him in Level 7 along with some of the other children in her class who started there. The fact that she excluded him from reading activities for the entire first quarter of the school year now placed him at a disadvantage behind the children who had skills similar to his when school started back in September. Now, several months later, the school prevented his placement with the other children because those children had progressed too far along in the Level 7 reading book. I could not understand why she brought the test scores to this meeting. If, in fact, she tested Gregory at the beginning of the school year, why did she not mention the scores on previous occasions when I specifically questioned why she excluded Gregory from her reading groups.

After she finished her presentation of those test results, we proceeded to the topic of Gregory's progress in his new reading group. Mrs Spears, his reading teacher, gave a positive report on Gregory's reading progress and commented that he completed his assignments on time. I had mixed emotions about the report. Hearing about Gregory's progress made me glad, but Gregory had finished only one unit in his new reading book after three weeks. The principal, during a previous conversation, said Level 7 should take only about six weeks to complete. The Principal answered my concern by explaining that the new group was slower paced.

Impromptu Visit

A few days after the meeting with the principal and teachers about Gregory's progress, I made an impromptu visit to Wren Lake School. Instead of going to the main entrance, I entered the building using an entrance off the parking lot. As I walked down the hall, I noticed a large room with some colorful oversized building blocks and some other toys in it. There were some Black children in the room, but they seemed too old to be playing with toys and blocks at school.

I proceeded down the hall. First, I visited Mrs, Kieper's classroom and took an empty seat to observe. The children were involved in various activities. Gregory, on the other hand, sat idle. He straightened and restraightened items at his desk. He walked over to one of the book shelves, pulled out a book, looked at it and then put it back on the shelf. He then went back to his desk to straighten and restraighten it again.

After a short period of time elapsed, Mrs Kieper came over to me and explained that Gregory appeared to have nothing to do because he was waiting for the other teacher to send for him for his reading group. I asked Mrs. Kieper to ignore my presence in the classroom.

Next, I went over to Mrs. Spears' classroom. She approached me right away. I requested that she ignore my presence in the classroom. I observed that the children in the class were working with a star. They were placing eight "s" words in the star.

After a period of time, Mrs. Spears sent one of the children to Mrs. Kieper's room to get Gregory. When Gregory came in, Mrs. Spears took him to a table near the middle of the room. She gave him a sheet of paper with a star on it. It was not unlike the one the other children were working with when I entered the room. She told him to think up eight "s" words that related to the season. (This was the winter season.) He needed to spell the "s" words that he came up with.

Mrs. Spears urged him several times, "Think, think, another, another!".

Then she prompted him, "Now, how do you spell s-l-e-i-g-h?" This went on for several minutes until he came up with and spelled the eight "s" words. The rest of the class continued to work on their stars while she worked with Gregory, but they became distracted.

The Truth Revealed

At the end of the period, she dismissed the children to go to some other activity. I took that opportunity to talk with Mrs. Spears.

"How is Gregory doing in reading?", I asked.

"Well", she said, "he's having a tough time. Did you see how hard it was for him to come up with the "s" words?".

"Yes, I noticed", I told her, "but, I don't understand why you took him aside to work on that by himself." "When did the other children come up with the words?", I asked.

She explained that since the other children are in her class all of the time, they came up with the words the previous day as a reading activity. I pointed out to her that with over 20 children in the class, some of them didn't have to come up with or spell any of the eight words. However, Gregory had to come up with and spell all eight words by himself and within only a few minutes.

I asked her why, since this was a reading activity, Gregory did not come up with the words with the members of his reading group. She explained that Gregory's reading group had never met. She told me the group had two other children in it. One was a girl who had medical problems and rarely came to school. The other was a Spanish boy who did not speak English. I thanked Mrs. Spears for her time and the extra effort she put forth to work with Gregory.

I felt wretched. I was not sure what I expected to learn by dropping in, but this was unsuspected. I went straight to the principal's office and confronted him with the fact that he placed Gregory in a non-existent reading group. I told him that it was unrealistic for anyone to expect Mrs. Spears to give Gregory a private reading session while over twenty other children went unsupervised. I emphasized that the likelihood she could adequately teach Gregory under those circumstances was slim to none.

Their failure to place Gregory in a reading group from the start of school so that he could progress along with the other children at the same level continued to puzzle me. I wanted to know what they expected to happen to Gregory when they kept him out of the reading groups. Did they plan to exclude him from reading for the entire school year? And then what???

I reminded Mr. Palmer that Gregory had been in a reading group at Live Oak Elementary where the teacher reported that he read well. Did they get a different report? I questioned, but I didn't get any real answers. Mr. Palmer promised to check into the reading placement situation and get back to me with answers to my questions.

During this period, I contacted a private school, also, located on the east side of Elgin. I took Gregory out of school for the better part of a day for a battery of admission tests. Later, on the appointment date set, we met with one of the school administrators. He advised us of their policy which prevents them from admitting students who are not doing well at their current school and who are not recommended by their current school. This information disappointed me.

A few days later, I went back to Gregory's school for a conference with Mr. Palmer in an effort to find out what they planned to do about teaching Gregory to read. I arrived early in order to talk to Mrs. Spears about the reading material and skills she covered with Gregory since she became his reading teacher. Mrs. Spears refused to talk to me because she said I got her into trouble when she talked to me before about Gregory.

Disappointed by her refusal, I waited for my meeting with the Principal. At the appointed time, we met and Mr. Palmer informed me that a decision had been made. Gregory would be placed in an existing reading group in Mrs. Kieper's classroom.

Several days later, I went to the school to see how Gregory was doing. Mrs. Kieper said he was not doing well in the group where he was placed. I asked her to provide me with classroom material such as word list and work sheet exercises so I could help Gregory learn and improve on the skills that she taught in class. She said that because the children completed all of their work in class, she did not have any material to give me. She suggested that any books I had at home would do just as well for helping him. When I left, I felt that Mrs. Kieper was not very cooperative or truthful about Gregory's reading dilemma.

The school year was very trying for me, and I was not sure Gregory would ever recover from it. Especially, since I was not sure he had totally recovered from what happened to him at Live Oak Elementary during his Kindergarten year. The two situations were very similar. In both cases, the teachers removed Gregory from the classroom to do nothing while they taught his classmates.

A few weeks into the second half of the school year, we received a note from Mrs Kieper. In the note, she said she was very sorry we felt she had not been fair to Gregory. I am not sure how else she expected us to feel. Also, she mentioned a Mrs Mitchell of whom I had not heard; however, when I talked with Mrs Mitchell about Gregory's progress, she told me that Mrs Kieper was the one who worked with him. The text of the note Mrs. Kieper sent may be seen on the next page.

At the end of the school year, Mrs. Kieper suggested that I consider having Gregory repeat the second grade. I did not want Gregory to repeat the second grade. Mrs. Kieper had intentionally harmed Gregory academically and destroyed his confidence about his ability to learn along with his classmates.

January 19, 1979

Mr. and Mrs. Darkins,

I am truly sorry that you have been displeased with me as Greg's teacher. This has been my first year as a 2nd grade teacher, and my most difficult task has been the assessment of each child's abilities and finding the proper instructional level for each. Since September I have worked very, very hard to do my very best to provide a quality education for all children in my room. I can do no more than that.

I hope that you will work ~~with~~ with Mrs. Mitchell for Greg's benefit. Mrs. Mitchell is a very capable teacher, and is more experienced than I.

If Greg has been unhappy, he has not shown it at school. He is well-liked and has many friends in all 3 classes.

Sincerely,   Alice Kieper

The Truth Revealed

Chris at Young's Corner

During the Summer before Gregory's Second Grade school year at Wren Lake Elementary, we enrolled Chris in Young's Corner for day care. In the Fall, Chris attended the Junior Kindergarten class there. Near the end of the Junior Kindergarten year at Young's Corner, the teachers tested the children. The school announced the test results and made appointments for the parents to review the test scores.

Ann Celler, the school's director, reviewed Chris' test with me. She gave me the form that contained the test areas as well as the teachers response to each question. There were a couple of areas that I felt we needed to discuss. The report indicated that Chris could not effectively use scissors or tie his shoes. I pointed out to Mrs. Celler that Chris wore shoes that needed to be tied every day. I purposely bought him shoes with shoestrings instead of velcro fasteners so he would learn to tie his shoes, and I didn't tie them for him each day. At school, they took their shoes off for nap time. They put them back on at the end of nap time and his shoes had to be tied. I asked how they could think he could not tie his shoes when he had to do it there everyday. I wasn't sure what problem he was having with the scissors, but he used them at home with ease. Also, the work he brought home from school, that required the use of scissors, did not show that he had difficulty with using them at school either. I did not want his record to show that he could not do things that he did every day. Ann Celler said it was just a test and nothing to worry about. Again, I let her know that I did not want a report that was clearly incorrect in his file no matter how insignificant they felt it was.

The teacher retested Chris on the areas I questioned. The teacher actually asked him to tie his shoes in her presence instead of relying on what she thought he could do. He tied his shoes with no problem. Ann Celler made a note at the bottom of the report to indicate that Chris sometimes asked others to tie his shoes for him and this led the teacher to believe he could not tie his own shoes. She, also, retested him with the scissors and found

49

his cutting was smooth rather than choppy as initially indicated. She made corrections to the report for the retested items. This report was the closest thing we got to a report card from the Junior Kindergarten class. (See Ann Celler's note below.)

* Chris has been asking other children to tie his shoes for him, which lied us to believe he could not tie.

Program Director

4
Waiting for a Change

In an effort to assure that Gregory would do well and not be removed from class during the next school year, I worked with him during the summer. We ordered the Science Reading Lab (SRA) learning materials in an attempt to get some structured material to work with instead of using library books and workbooks we bought at the store. As I worked with Gregory, I realized that I needed to be careful not to put too much pressure on him. To my dismay, I noticed that the pressure I placed on Gregory was driving a wedge between us. The casual learning time we use to share and enjoy was now more serious on my part and no longer fun for him.

I suspected that what was happening to Gregory was also happening to other Black and minority children who attended Wren Lake Elementary School and a number of situation confirmed my suspicions. At the church we attended, I met a Black couple who lived in an older section of our subdivision. They had two daughters. Their elder daughter, older than Gregory, had a beautiful voice and sang solos in the choir at church. She attended Wren Lake school as well. On one occasion, her family invited me to a celebration at their home. In the course of a discussion, I ventured to ask if they were having any problems with the school or if they noticed that their daughters were not being taught along with the other children. The girl's father became indignant at my suggestion that the school might not teach his daughter. He said his daughter made straight A's in school, and if my son was having problems, perhaps, I should look at my son or myself. He was upset. I told him that I was glad to hear his daughter was doing so well in school and let the subject drop.

Less than a year later, I ran into the mother and their daughters at the grocery store. We stood outside and chatted while she waited for her husband to pick them up. She told me their elder daughter had started having problems with her grades in school. The daughter's teacher informed them that she was not reading at grade level and needed special help. She and her husband were confused because this daughter had always done so well in school. The father was disappointed and upset with the daughter for not bringing home good reports anymore.

The Brazilian lady who baby sat Gregory told me her son was recommended for retention by his teacher. Ronald's teacher said that he simply did not read well enough and his mother considered letting him repeat the Second Grade. When her twin daughters were old enough for Kindergarten, school officials told her they were not ready for regular Kindergarten. She sent them to two separate special schools provided by the district. The district advised her that the girls should go to separate schools because they didn't think it was good for twins to be together in school. The family juggled going to functions at three different schools and the functions were usually on the same evening.

Gregory in Third Grade

The next year Gregory continued at Wren Lake Elementary as a third grader. As far as how well he was doing in school, I never really felt comfortable that I knew. Even after conferences with his teacher, I wasn't sure. Gregory's Third Grade teacher reported that he was doing satisfactory work. He completed Level 9 in the Holt, Rhinhart and Winston reading series by the end of the Third Grade. This was still below grade level for reading. However, I was glad that he had made some progress in school. I got the idea he enjoyed the Third Grade. At the end of the school year, Gregory was promoted to the Fourth Grade.

Chris in Kindergarten

The next year, Janet, the neighbor who kept Gregory, agreed to keep Chris before and after school also. We registered Chris for Kindergarten at Wren Lake Elementary School. During the spring, the Kindergarten teachers held a meeting to introduce parents to their Kindergarten program. They explained what the children would be expected to do during the school year and what a typical day in Kindergarten would be like. Chris had been exposed to all of the items they said they would teach. I left the orientation feeling that Chris would not have any problems meeting or exceeding expectations in Kindergarten.

Chris' Kindergarten teacher was Mrs. Whitney. Chris was the only Black child in the class of about 21 students. Chris appeared to be doing well in school. All of the paperwork he brought home was graded with good, excellent or stars on it. There was no reason for me to think he might be slow or was not doing well.

Then one day Chris came home from school wanting to talk to me. He said, "Mom, you need to go to the school and talk to Mrs. Whitney. She is teaching some of the children to read, but she's not teaching me to read."

I reflected for a moment and then asked Chris if he was sure that Mrs. Whitney was teaching some of the children to read. I told him that during orientation, the Kindergarten teachers told us what things they would teach and reading was not one of them. They said they would teach letters, colors and numbers to prepare the children for reading in First Grade.

"Well," he said, "Mrs. Whitney is teaching some of the children to read."

He paused slightly and then said, "I told her that I want to learn to read too, but she told me to go sit down. So, you need to talk to Mrs. Whitney and tell her that I want to be in one of the groups she is teaching to read."

A Name I Can't Read

I looked at Chris for a few moments and then told him that I would talk to Mrs. Whitney about the reading when I went to the school for our conference. Mrs. Whitney and I already had an appointment set for the next week to discuss Chris's progress in school. As far as I knew, he was not having a problem, but it was conference time, and I made it a point to schedule a conference with his teacher in order to get a feeling for how things were going.

I went to school for my conference with Mrs. Whitney as planned. Both of the Kindergarten teachers were conducting conferences in the same room. I was near the last to be seen as I scheduled for the latest time I could get. Mrs. Whitney had a lot of praise for Chris' work and for his behavior. His progress report was very good. As we finished talking about Chris' progress, I informed Mrs. Whitney that Chris had observed her teaching some of the children to read. I told her that Chris was anxious to learn to read and wanted to be included in one of the reading groups.

"Oh no, Mrs. Darkins, we are not teaching these children to read.", she chuckled and said in a matter of fact manner. "It is all we can do to cover the skills we have listed here to cover."

She showed me a copy of the sheet listing the skills they planned to cover in Kindergarten. It was the same list we were shown during Kindergarten orientation.

"We can't possibly teach these Kindergarten children to read.", she continued.

That night, after the conference, I told Chris that Mrs. Whitney said they were not teaching the Kindergarten children to read.

"I see her teaching children to read, and they have reading books just for learning to read.", he said. "I know she's teaching children to read. Humph.", he added while gazing at me.

He continued to look at me quizzically as if to ask, "Aren't you going to do something?"

Waiting For a Change

I sat there reflecting, but I knew there was no more that I would do. His teacher had denied that she was teaching children to read.

By this time Chris had memorized some of his favorite bedtime story books that I read to him night after night. He took books into the bathroom with him and recited stories from memory, while turning the pages at pretty close to the appropriate time. The first time I heard him doing this, I listened for a while and then eased over to see if he was really reading. I soon realized that he was reciting from memory. He was tickled to think he almost fooled me.

Guilt about not teaching Chris to read overwhelmed me. Here my child was literally begging to be taught to read, and I had not taught him. I figured I could teach him to read, so I decided to teach Chris to read. By now it was springtime, and I planned to start teaching Chris to read as soon as school let out for the summer.

My big concern was what materials to use and where to obtain that material. Chris and Gregory had lots of children's story books, but they contained a lot of different types of words that required the learning of various reading skills before Chris would be ready to read them. Chris knew the letters of the alphabet and some words that began with the letters. But, I didn't know how that related to where he should start reading from books off the shelf. I felt the need to find a reading series that started at the beginning and provided the skill building material to use as Chris progressed through the series. I wanted to find a structured reading program for the task of teaching Chris to read.

I looked for reading material at book stores. I went to the Gail Borden Public Library to see if they had or knew of any material appropriate for what I wanted to do. The lady at the library said they left the teaching of children up to the schools, and would not have any material packaged for that purpose on the shelves. I perused the library, but did not find anything that was quite what I was looking for.

A Name I Can't Read

As I continued to look for material, I heard about the Ladybird Key Word reading series and where to find some of the books. I found some of the books, but the workbooks and other supportive materials were not available at that location. I wrote to the publisher for information on how to order the material. They directed me to the proper place and I ordered several of the primers and the workbooks that went with them. I hoped the material would be back before summer came because I wanted to start the lessons as soon as the kids were out of school.

Metropolitan Readiness Test Result

Near the end of the school year, the school notified us that the results of the Metropolitan Readiness test, given to all Kindergarten children, were ready for parents to review. We went to the school on the day and time indicated and gathered with all of the other Kindergarten parents in one big room. As the test booklets were passed out, the principal explained that booklets with a "10" written on the cover indicated that the child taking the test scored in the top ten percentile of all children taking the test. Chris' booklet had a "10" on the cover. The school principal went on to explain that the results of the test were used as a factor in determining how well a child is expected to do in school. He said that a child, scoring in the top "50" percentile is expected to complete Level 7 in the Holt, Rhinhart and Winston reading material by the end of the First Grade. We were excited that Chris had done so well.

I Taught Chris to Read

Finally, the reading material arrived and during the summer, following his Kindergarten year, I taught Chris to read. Chris sat for his lessons without a problem. When he was outside playing with his friends, he came in when he thought it was time for his lesson. Even when he had company, he made it a point to break for his lesson. Chris wanted to learn to read and was, therefore, easy to teach.

Waiting For a Change

I kept his lesson time down to less than an hour. As a guide in conducting the lessons, I used the parents booklet provided with the materials. As a part of his lesson, he reviewed words, learned new words, reviewed the words again. He did the reading and workbook exercises that went along with the lessons. We didn't purchase the flash cards for the key words introduced in his lessons. Instead, we used index cards and a roll of continuous paper. I put new words on index cards which we used on the day the words were introduced. After that, the words were added to the words on the continuous form of words introduced during previous lessons. This kept the words he had already studied together for review. Chris' rapid progress amazed me, and I think he was amazed too. One thing for sure, Chris felt good about learning to read books.

Our neighbor, who lived across the street, had a little girl the same age as Chris. Her daughter, Connie, went to Wren Lake Elementary for Kindergarten the same as Chris. When my neighbor heard that I was giving Chris reading lessons, she wanted to know why. I told her that Chris really wanted to learn to read so I decided to teach him. She said the school had taught her daughter to read from the beginner readers, but she guessed they didn't do that for all the children. I told her that I guessed not because they had not started teaching Chris to read.

The summer quickly came to an end. In less than a month school would open to begin the next school year. I looked for a new baby sitter to care for the children before and after school. The neighbor who cared for them wanted to do some other things now that the twins, her youngest children, were old enough for school.

A Tutor is Found

Toward the end of the summer before Gregory's Fourth Grade school year and Chris' First Grade year, the Homeowner's Association had a big party on the grounds near the clubhouse. At the party, I met a couple who lived in a newer section of our subdivision. The wife, Shelly, worked as a school teacher within the same school district as the one where Gregory and Chris went to school. Shelly was pregnant with their second child and their older daughter had some medical problems which required that she have a number of surgeries performed. Since the pregnancy was going to cause Shelly to miss some time from work, she planned to take the entire school year off from teaching to take care of her daughters medical problems. She planned to return to work at the end of the next summer. She was looking for a couple of children to care for before and after school. She planned to schedule her doctor appointments and those of her daughter so that they would not conflict with the baby sitting. I jumped at the chance to have her watch Gregory and Chris. Our current baby sitter had already expressed an interest in doing other things now that her twin daughters were school age.

Shelly, agreed to care for Gregory and Chris before and after school. The children would still be able to walk across the playground to get to school. With the child care details settled, I asked Shelly if she would consider tutoring Gregory and Chris in reading and math. She agreed to tutor the boys, and I felt a tremendous weight lifted from my shoulders. Meeting Shelly made me very happy. I felt that she was a God send.

Shelly wanted to coordinate her tutoring work with the school to make sure she assisted the boys where the school determined they needed extra help. She knew the district provided skill building material and she would look to the school for the materials needed to assist my children in areas where their skills were weak. She planned to supplement the tutoring material from the school with material she already owned or could obtain from other sources. I took the SRA (Science Reading Lab) material over to Shelly in case it could be used.

After school started, Shelly wrote to the children's teachers to inform them that she would be tutoring Gregory and Chris. She let them know that she wanted on-going information about their expected school work in order to address specific skills in her tutoring as needed. The school simply did not respond to Shelly's request.

Shelly obtained some level testing material for the Holt, Rhinhart and Winston reading program through some of her contacts in the district. She tested Gregory and placed him in level 10 of Holt, Rhinhart and Winston. This happened to be where he left off the previous school year at the end of Third Grade.

Shelly started having a problem with Gregory shortly after she began tutoring him. After his snack, he wanted to go outside to play with his friends who usually gathered outside and waited for him. He did not want to sit down and do the work she planned for him. However, Gregory learned that the sooner he got started on the work that Shelly gave him, the sooner he would finish and the sooner he could go outside to play with his friends. Shelly said that Gregory started doing his work immediately after he finished his snack when he had learned that was the only way to get out of the house. Pouting did not work.

Later, when I got to see the wonderful, well put together tree house that Gregory, Michael Genie, and Hsung Siu built in the wooded area behind the cul-de-sac facing ours, I understood why he was in such a rush to go out and play.

Shelly, also, worked with Chris. She started him off at the point where I had him in the Ladybird Key Word Reading Series. In addition, she used the SRA reading kit as she saw fit. After a few days of tutoring Chris, Shelly told me he was doing very well. She related that he was ready to start his lessons as soon as he came in from school. He eagerly practiced the new words, did the word reviews, read the text and worked on the workbook exercises. He then went on to do the math exercises she gave him. Because he started working right away, he finished the work and had time to play before I picked him and his brother up in the evening. I was happy that Chris continued working so diligently on his desire to learn to read.

5
A Cry for Help

A Black man, Mr. Burns, became Gregory's teacher in the fourth grade. Shortly after school started, I talked to Mr. Burns about Gregory's reading placement. He told me Gregory really needed to improve his reading in order to be at grade level. He said Gregory had been tested for reading and scored 60 percent on Holt Level 10 and it was recommended that he be placed in Level 9. I told Mr. Burns that Gregory completed Level 9 the year before and received a satisfactory report. I, also, informed Mr. Burns that Gregory had a tutor who wanted to work with him and the school to help Gregory master any skills they felt he needed help with. After my conversation with Mr. Burns, I wrote him a letter to recap our discussion. (The text of a letter written to Mr. Burns early in the school year may be seen on the next pages.)

A Name I Can't Read

Phone: ......
576-5848 days
OR 952-5193

Elgin, Illinois 60120
9/10/80

District 446

CC: Mr   ,Principal

Subject: Reading Placement for
Gregory Darkins - 4th Grade Student

Dear Mr.

Pursuant to our conversation of September, 9, 1980 regarding the reading placement of Gregory Darkins. You advised that as Gregory scored 60% on the level 10 reading test for holt it is recommended that he be placed in holt Reading level 9.

We respect the need for school guidelines in the reading placement of children. However, Gregory was in holt reading level 9 last year and at last report he was doing satisfactory work at that level. We strongly feel that to have him repeat that same material again this year would not provide a positive affect on his interest and concentration levels.

We are also opposed to Gregory being shuffled in and out of the classroom from reading Holt to reading special books as has been the pattern for the two years that Gregory has attended Lords Park School.

With a 60% reading score on the Holt level 10 reading test, we feel that Gregory should be placed at level 10 in the school's normal reading series (Holt). This would provide Gregory with new material to develop his reading skill and would also provide for learning challenge.

This year Gregory is in a unique position in that he will be tutored by a professional teacher in the field of elementary education. We

Page 3 of 3

Know that in order for him to take the best advantage of this situation he must be placed at a reading level where there is potential for growth. Level 10 in Holt's basic reading system would provide that potential at this time.

We realize that it is early in the school year. However, the early placement of Gregory at a suitable and beneficial reading level should minimize the possibility of displacement later in the school year.

Gregory's tutor is cognizant of the importance of correlating her efforts with those of the school in order to maximize the benefits of the tutoring effort. For this reason we need to be kept informed of Gregory's placement and changes in that placement made by the school.

Please let us hear from you within the next week. Our address and phone numbers are listed on page 1.

Sincerely,

Claudia Dirkins   Claudia M. Dirkins

A Cry For Help

Later, when I talked to Mr. Burns again about Gregory's reading placement, he informed me that Gregory was not in his class for reading. He told me he did not personally do the testing on Gregory for placement in reading because that was determined by other members of the school's staff.

I checked further about Gregory's reading placement and found that the school had placed him in an alternate textbook. That alternate textbook was equivalent to Holt Level 4. The school dropped Gregory's reading placement down 5 levels below where he read at the end of the Third Grade.

I questioned Mr. Palmer about why they dropped Gregory's reading instructional level down to Level 4 after his performance report from the past school year indicated that he successfully completed Level 9. He informed me that they gave Gregory a test which showed that he should be in Level 4, so they placed him in Level 4.

Out of sheer frustration, I went to the school district superintendent's office seeking help regarding the way Gregory was being shuffled around at Wren Lake Elementary. I expressed my frustration with the way Gregory was dropped to a level equivalent to Level 4 in reading although he successfully completed Level 9 the year before. I, also, expressed dismay with the fact that not so much as a word was spoken to Gregory's father or me about this decision having been made or implemented. I related to the superintendent that Gregory had been excluded from the reading groups at Wren Lake Elementary in the past and had, now, been taken out of the reading series used by Wren Lake Elementary altogether. (The Level 4 book they placed him in was published by Houghton Miflin instead of Holt, Rhinhart and Winston which was used by Wren Lake Elementary). The Superintendent assured me that he would check with the school and get back in touch with me.

By this time, Gregory had managed to complete Holt Level 10 with his tutor.

Independent Testing for Gregory and Chris

Meanwhile, my husband and I felt very uncomfortable about the academic development of our children. By this time Gregory was in the Fourth Grade and Chris was in the First Grade. We decided to have them tested in an effort to see if any problems would surface that we did not know about. We wanted to see how they would do on a battery of test conducted outside the school system. After calling around for testing services, we discovered Warren Associates in Chicago.

We took Gregory and Chris to Warren Associates for consultation and testing. They conducted the testing over two Saturdays. They administered the Iowa test and also did level testing in Holt, Rhinhart and Winston.

The Warren Associates report indicated that Gregory showed a readiness for Holt Level 11 and not Level 4 as the school put him in. The testing also showed that Gregory's understanding of math concepts exceeded his ability to solve math problems that required reading and interpretation. They suggested that this related to a deficient reading development and could correct as the reading development level increased.

As for Chris, the testing showed that he exceeded his grade level in all areas. The testing indicated a readiness for Holt reading Level 8, instead of the Level 2 material the school placed Chris in. Additionally, it pointed out that Chris was ready for an accelerated math and language program because he scored well above his school grade level.

We had a copy of the report from Warren Associates sent to the school superintendent and to Wren Lake Elementary. If the school did any additional testing on Gregory, during this period, they did not share it with us. After receiving the test results from Warren Associates, the school wrote to say that they would test Gregory and place him according to their testing because they did not want him to be frustrated in a reading group above his level.

The text of the Warren Associates report regarding Gregory and Chris appears on the following pages.

WARREN ASSOCIATES

8023 S. Marshfield Avenue
Chicago, Illinois 60620
February 12, 1981

Gregory and Christopher Darkins were tested on two successive Saturdays. Neither the Darkins children nor their parents were known to me personally prior to our meeting for the initial test session. After a brief conference both parents left, and returned when all testing was completed.

Gregory and Christopher were aware of the fact that they were to be tested and expressed a readiness for same. Christopher was far more animated than his older brother, both verbally and physically.

Gregory completed the timed tests in all areas shortly before the required time limits, while Christopher completed all areas tested well before the required time limits. In accordance with the prescribed directions for each test area, Gregory worked with no assistance as required.

In the Reading Comprehension, Word Recognition II, and Mathematics Computation portions, Christopher was also required to work with no assistance. All other areas were administered with the tester reading each item, and the student marking his response immediately.

67

WARREN ASSOCIATES

8023 S. Marshfield Avenue
Chicago, Illinois 60620
February 12, 1981

At the request of Mr. and Mrs. Clarence Darkins, their
sons Gregory Gerard Darkins, age 9, and Christopher Oji Darkins,
age 6 were given a battery of standardized tests, and the
Holt Placement Inventory.

The Darkins expressed an interest in determining the academic
achievement of their sons to date, as well as identifying areas
of particular strength and of need.

The tests were administered on January 31, 1981 and
February 7, 1981. This is a report of the results of those tests.

GREGORY DARKINS

IOWA TEST OF BASIC SKILLS, Level 9 Form 6
Houghton Mifflin Company

TEST	GRADE EQUIVALENT	PERCENTILE (MID-YEA
VOCABULARY	3.5	52
READING COMPREHENSION	3.5	51
MATHEMATICS CONCEPTS	4.1	72
MATHEMATICS PROBLEMS	2.7	26

HOLT PLACEMENT INVENTORY: SILENT READING

LEVEL	SCORE
9	100%
10	100%

In every instance, Christopher's test results indicate achievement far beyond the Mid-Year of Grade 1, except when asked to recognize words by sight. It is clear that his sight vocabulary is lacking. It must be noted however, that in each instance of an incorrect response, Christopher used his very strong phonetic skills in choosing an answer. This was the case in both the Comprehensive Test of Basic Skills; a standardized test, and in the Holt Placement Silent Reading Inventory.

Gregory's test results were consistent in all areas except Mathematics Concepts. This may be the case because it was the first test completed during the second testing session, while the Mathematics Problems test followed the Reading Comprehension section during the first testing period. It is also probable that Gregory's achievement in terms of concepts exceeds his ability to read and respond to mathematics problems which require both reading and interpretation prior to actual mathematics operations. Gregory completed the problems section in less than half the time allowed and seemed to give up on the test.

RECOMMENDATIONS

Christopher's test results indicate his readiness for reading at Holt Level 8, accompanied by a strong program of drill in the Dolch Sight Vocabulary as well as the Holt Vocabulary up to and including Level 8. He is also ready for an accelerated mathematics curriculum, as his achievement is nearly two years beyond his current grade placement.

Gregory's test results indicate his readiness for reading at Holt Level 11, accompanied by a supportive program in reading comprehension such as those offered by Science Research Associates Reading Laboratories. His mathematics needs are in the area of reading and interpreting word problems. More practice in these skillsshould enable him to achieve with efficiency equal to his abilities in terms of mathematics concepts.

CHRISTOPHER DARKINS

COMPREHENSIVE TESTS OF BASIC SKILLS, EXPANDED EDITION
Level B Form S
McGraw-Hill Publishing Company

TEST	TOTAL	GRADE EQUIVALENT	PERCENTILE (MID-YEAR
READING	62	1.8	88
Letter Sounds	20		85
Word Recognition I	11		76
Comprehension	20		85
Word Recognition II	11		78
LANGUAGE	32	2.5	95
Language I	16		98
Language II	16		80
MATHEMATICS	54	2.9	99
Concepts	24		99
Computation	30		98
TOTAL BATTERY	148	2.0	94

HOLT PLACEMENT INVENTORY : SILENT READING

LEVEL	SCORE
6	100%
7	100%

A Name I Can't Read

Chris in First Grade

I felt anxious when Chris started First Grade because of the situations we experienced with the school failing to teach Gregory. Also, I felt anxious because Chris had expressed that he was not being taught to read along with his classmates while he was in Kindergarten. I wanted to be aware of Chris' academic placement early in the school year. For that reason, I visited Wren Lake Elementary during the first week to observe in the classroom. I followed the prescribed procedure by stopping at the Principal's office first. I told Mr. Palmer that I wanted to observe Chris' class. He informed me that they were still trying to get organized and the teachers needed more time to become familiar with the children. He asked me to return when the school had Open House. He said the teachers would explain how things were going and show me the classroom at that time.

Mr. Palmer walked down the hall with me. When we got to Chris' classroom, he peered through the glass in the door. He pointed out that the children were busy taking placement test to determine where they should be placed for instruction. I looked through the glass and saw that the children were busy with paperwork. Chris had his head bowed over some papers too. I agreed to return on the day of the Open House.

I returned to Wren Lake Elementary on the night open house was scheduled. We were introduced to the teachers in general assembly and then we were dismissed to go to the classrooms. The teachers gave a presentation about how they planned to conduct the class during the school year. They showed us the textbooks the children were using and explained that all children would not have the same textbook. The teachers told us that the textbook a child used depended on the level where that particular child was being taught.

After the presentations were over, we, the parents, were invited to find our child's desk and see the textbooks where our child was placed. I found Chris' desk and looked through the books that were on his desk. I saw a large picture book with Level

2 on the front cover. As I looked through the pages, I noticed that he was near the beginning of the book. He didn't have any one of the small reading textbooks the teachers had shown us earlier during the presentation. I glanced around the room and saw that each child's desk that I looked on had a Level 3 or above textbooks setting on it.

The fact that Chris did not have a reading textbook concerned me. Based upon my understanding of what the teachers said during the presentation, I felt sure this meant that Chris was not being taught to read in school. My mind returned to the ordeal suffered upon finding that my oldest son was not being taught and a gripping fear began to rise within my being. I became determined to hear why Chris' teacher had not placed him in a reading textbook and started teaching him reading. Some of the parents had already lined up to talk to the teacher. I got in line.

A Spanish women stood in front of me in line. Tears ran down her face as she pleaded with Mrs. Burton to give her son a chance to show he could learn well enough at his grade level to remain in Wren Lake Elementary instead of being bused to one of the special schools provided by the district. Although, I didn't know the special school the lady was referring to, I thought it might be one of the ones that Chris and Gregory's previous baby sitter's twin daughters were sent to. (Her daughters were sent to special schools provided by the district because the school felt they were not ready for the regular classroom.) No matter how much the Spanish lady pleaded, Mrs. Burton did not budge. She emphatically told the lady it was best for her child to be in the Special Education program.

Finally, my opportunity to speak with the teacher came. I questioned Mrs. Burton about why Chris was in a picture book and why he did not have one of the reading books that she had shown us earlier. Mrs. Burton gave no specific reason but stated that she placed Chris where he left off the last school year. I asked her how Chris did on the placement test given by her at the beginning of the school year. She denied that any testing had been done and reiterated that she had merely started Chris where he left off the previous year.

The teachers had explained to us earlier that, with the exception of quick questions, we needed to sign up for appointments in order to talk with the teachers about the progress of individual students. I signed up for an appointment to talk with Mrs. Burton.

Finally, the appointment day arrived. My husband and I both attended the conference. Mrs. Burton sat behind her desk with her arms folded and looked at us blankly as we approached. I felt like we were about to engage in a conversation with a brick wall. We took the seats that were in front of her desk. Mrs. Burton did not say a word but waited for us to start the conversation. We explained our concern about her placing Chris at a pre-reading level. (He was placed at the beginning of a Level 2 textbook and Level 3 was the first reading level.) We told Mrs. Burton we were surprised by Chris' current reading level placement. We explained to Mrs. Burton that during his Kindergarten year, Chris scored in the top ten percentile of all children taking the Metropolitan Readiness Test, and consequently we expected him to be placed at a higher reading level. Mrs. Burton sat without apparent interest while we talked. Then she told us that she felt Chris was doing very well in her class.

"But, you're not teaching him to read." I spoke the obvious.

She looked at us in a very matter of fact way and went on to tell us that she was quite pleased with where she had placed Chris in her class. At that point, she kept looking at us as if to indicate that the conference was over and there was nothing more to discuss. Our conference ended.

We left Mrs. Burton and went to the principal's office to explain our situation to him. We advised him that we had talked to Mrs. Burton about the fact that she was not teaching Chris to read. We reminded Mr. Palmer of Chris' ranking among the top ten on the Metropolitan Readiness Test and how he, himself, said the results of the test were used as a factor in determining how well children are expected to do in school. Based on the fact that Chris scored in the top 10 percentile, we told Mr. Palmer that we expected Chris to be among those being taught to read. Mr. Palmer told us that he would have to review the situation and talk to Chris' teacher before he could intelligently discuss Chris' reading placement with us. We set an appointment for the following week.

I returned to school to talk to the principal the following week, as scheduled. He informed me that he had talked with Mrs. Burton. He said that I needed to understand that, although, some children can score well on test, they are not always ready to read. He said that children who fall into this category should not be forced to read until they are ready. He said that he and Mrs. Burton had come to the conclusion that Chris fell into this category and simply was not ready to read.

I was shocked by the Principal's explanation of why the teacher was not teaching Chris to read. This was not the response I expected to hear. I did not expect to be told that Chris was not being taught to read because he was not ready to read; especially since he ranked in the top 10 percentile on the readiness test. I told Mr. Palmer that not only was Chris ready to read, but he was reading already. Mr. Palmer appeared surprised.

"What do you mean, he reads?", he said as he raised his eyebrows and looked at me scrutinizing.

I explained that Chris had been reading for several months using books that I bought for him. Mr. Palmer explained that he was trying to tell me that Chris was not ready to read from the schools reading material, which is different from the materials that you buy at the store. His explanation did not persuade me and I told him that the books I taught Chris from were designed for the purpose of teaching children to read. I told him that I started teaching Chris to read because he was eager to learn to read.

A Name I Can't Read

Mr. Palmer asked me to bring some of Chris' books to the school so that he could evaluate them. I told Mr. Palmer that I wouldn't bring Chris' books to the school because I wanted Chris to be taught from the reading books used by the school. Mr. Palmer said he'd look at the reading situation further and call me.

Before leaving the school, I asked Mr. Palmer how Chris scored on the test given during the first week of school. He denied that the school had tested the children.

Mr. Palmer called after a few weeks passed. He advised me that he and Mrs. Burton decided to continue Chris in reading at Level 2. I asked how far Chris had progressed and how long they expected him to remain in Level 2. He promised to check with Mrs. Burton and send me a note with answers to those questions. It was about the middle of the school year when I received the note. The note indicated that Chris was approximately half way through Level 2, considering that they would be skipping some of the pages. A copy of the note follows:

Dear Mrs. Darkins,
    We are approximately half-way through level 2, as there are certain pages in the book that we will be skipping.
            Mrs. ⸱⸱

Rec'd. Jan 5th

A Cry For Help

A Visit to the District

The realization that Chris would probably remain in Level 2 reading for the duration of the first grade both dismayed and frustrated me. He had proven his ability to learn by scoring in the top 10 percentile of all the children in the district on the Metropolitan Readiness test. Now all of his classmates had been allowed to surpass him because the teacher and the principal refused to teach him along with the other students. They wasted his time with busy work from a picture book.

Anguished and not knowing where else to turn, I went to the school district for help. Mr. Crow, the Superintendent, listened to what I had to say. He promised to check with the school and get back in touch with me. During that same visit, I talked to Mr. Crow about the reading problem we were having with Gregory. We waited for a response from the district.

It was during this time that we took Chris and Gregory to an independent testing service to get feedback from a source other than the school. The result of that testing was presented in Chapter 19. In the meantime, the baby sitter continued to work with Chris in reading and math.

Chris' reading placement situation caused me extreme personal stress, especially when I considered the problems we were already having with Gregory not being taught. If I ever had doubts about whether the school's failure to teach my children was intentional, I had no doubt now that it was intentional. Imagine a child scoring in the top 10 percentile on the Metropolitan Readiness Test and the teacher failing to teach him with the excuse that he is not ready to read. I knew that excuse did not apply to Chris because I had already taught him to read because of his readiness. We continued to wait for a response from the school district.

All the while, I felt the school was being unfair and that they were committing a crime by not teaching our children. In the mist of my stress and frustration, I contacted a lawyer to get an idea about what could be done. The lawyer was not optimistic and advised that it would be difficult to make a case and prove the school was at fault. He pointed out that by the time we went through the court system the children would be grown. He suggested that we find a way to send the children to some other school and not try to fight that battle. Chris had made friends with another Black child named Kevin. Kevin and his parents lived nearer to the school, but they did not send Kevin there. His mother said that after visiting the school they decided to send Kevin to a school near some people they knew outside the district. In dismay, I did not attempt to pursue solving our problems with the school through the legal system.

A few weeks passed before we received a call from the district Reading Coordinator. She advised us that her office had been informed of our concern about our sons not being taught reading at the appropriate level and they were already in contact with the school. They wanted to meet with us to discuss their decisions. They requested that we bring some of the books that Chris learned to read from at home because they wanted to evaluate the books and note them in their records.

At the meeting, the district Reading Coordinators advised us that they would conduct test to determine Chris' reading readiness and make recommendations based on those test results. The test would be conducted at Wren Lake Elementary during the regular school day. The district Reading Coordinator said she would make arrangements with the school and let us know the testing date. My husband advised Mr. Palmer and the reading coordinators that he wanted to observe the testing process. However, the Reading Coordinator who was going to do the actual testing, protested letting him observe. She said that if he observed, she would feel like he was looking over her shoulder. At this point, my husband became visibly upset. He raised his index finger, arched his eyebrows and gradually raised his voice as he spoke.

He said, "You people don't seem to understand; this is my child you're messing with, and you can be darn sure I'll be looking over your shoulder, and if I can not be there, you will not test.

Now, that's the bottom line." He paused, reared back in his chair. Then he sat erect and continued with emphasis, "I'm telling you; I'm tired of all this nonsense."

Mr. Palmer said, "Mr. Darkins, I am sure we can find a way for you to observe without disturbing the testing."

My husband said in exasperation, "I know you will. Thank you."

We were advised of the date and time for the testing and were told to make sure Chris was not aware that we were going to be at the school.

On the test day, Chris' dad could not attend the testing session at the school because of a work commitment. As it turned out the testing room had an observation area. The supervising Reading Coordinator from the district and I watched the testing in the observation area. We were already situated when Mrs. Curtis entered the testing area with Chris.

Mrs. Curtis started Chris off reading books published by Holt, Rhinhart and Winston which was the publisher used by the school. She required that Chris read a passage from the textbook and then answer questions from a sheet of questions based on the passage read.

Mrs. Curtis started testing Chris at Level 3 and proceeded to test him through Level 8 using the same evaluation process. Chris had no difficulty at all with Levels 3, 4 or 6 (personally, I don't recall Level 5). He read the passages and answered the questions asked. Before one of the levels, Mrs. Curtis asked Chris if he wanted her to tell him the word 'sister'. He said yes. After that, he went on to read the passage with no assistance and he answered all of the questions associated with the passage. At Level 8, Mrs. Curtis determined that she needed to read the passage to Chris. When she finished reading the passage, she asked Chris the questions associated with the passage and he answered all of the questions with no difficulty. Then, Mrs. Curtis had Chris read to her from one of his books from the Ladybird Key Word Reading Series. After that she introduced a series of word lists. The testing session was very long and even I became exhausted by it.

When the testing ended, the supervising reading coordinator advised me that the district would let us know their findings and recommendations after they reviewed the test results. A copy of the test results follow:

A Cry For Help

Christopher Darkins
Grade 1 Mary Whitney
Lords Park School

Examiner - Joanne Curtis
Date - February 4, 1981

Reason for Referral

Christopher's parents have been concerned about his reading in
the classroom as they believe he could be placed in a book at
a higher level in the Holt Basic Reading than his present level.
As he has been reading at home in the Ladybird Key Words Reading Scheme, a series of small story books designed to build
sight vocabulary, they believe that Holt Level 2 is inappro-
priate. The examiner agreed to assess Christopher's reading
as an aid to a determination of most appropriate instruction
for him in his classroom.

Background Information

Christopher's teacher says that he has been working on the Holt
Level 2 workbook activities to develop phonic skills. This has
been primarily recognition of beginning consonant sounds with
some work in using beginning consonant substitutions in word
bases, such as _ap, _en, _ed, _op, _ock. In addition, there
has been some instruction on recognition of ending consonant
sounds and short vowel sounds.

His kindergarten teacher told the examiner that she felt that
Christopher had shown "average" readiness skills for reading in
kindergarten. On the Metropolitan Readiness Tests administered
to Chris on April 2, 1980, he had a stanine score of 5 on the
Auditory Skills subtests, a stanine of 7 on Visual Skills, and
a stanine of 5 on Language Skills, giving a Pre-Reading Skills
Composite stanine score of 6. The kindergarten teacher stated
that she had felt much concern that he had been unable to express
his ideas or feelings freely. She said that he usually responded
to direct questions with single words or brief phrases.

The examiner observed Christopher in his classroom for approximately ten minutes on January 23. At that time his teacher was
explaining what the children were to do on an art project.
Christopher was looking at the teacher and seemed to be paying
attention to the instructions.

A Name I Can't Read

Christopher Darkins, continued

Behavioral Observations

In order that Mrs. Darkins might be able to observe the session
from the observation area of a special education classroom,
the testing took place after school. Christopher expressed
no concern when told the examiner would like to hear him read.
When he sat down at the table, the examiner showed him the
Holt books from which he would be reading and four books from
the Ladybird series (provided by Mrs. Darkins). When asked if
he knew the Ladybird books, he pointed out three he recognized.
Asked what he liked best about school, he responded with
"Reading."

The session began with a check on the words used in Holt Level
3 books that are introduced in Level 2. Chris said each word
on the list unhesitatingly and continued with the first twenty-
eight words of the Level 3 book. As Christopher had demonstrated that he knew at least some of the Holt vocabulary, the
examiner decided to administer the Oral Reading Inventory. The
inventory is given by asking the child to read a passage aloud
from a book and then answer questions about that passage.

When asked to read a short story "Open the Books" from Level 3,
he read fluently and answered the four literal questions confidently. This confident approach to the task continued as he
read passages from Levels 4, 5, and 6 even though he made a
few errors. His responses to questions were often one-word
with no elaboration.

When the question on a Level 4 passage was "Who wants to make
cookies?" he responded, "Jenny." The examiner had to ask, "Who
else wants to make cookies?" to get the rest of the correct response, "Jill."

Before reading the Level 5 passage, "Shep, the Sheep Dog,"
Chris was asked if he knows what a sheep dog does, to which
he responded "He helps the shepherd with his sheep." He had
some confusion on this passage as he sometimes read "sheep"
for "Shep," and "Shep" for "sheep."

When he read the passage from Level 6, he misread the word
"sister" as "shelter." The examiner supplied the word
"sister" which he recalled when he read it correctly four
lines later in the story. He answered the questions, but
again needed to have a question repeated to give the second
part of an answer.

- 3 -

Christopher Darkins, continued

Chris had difficulty reading the Level 7 passage. As he read,
he put his face closer and closer to the page, stopped several
times, made substitutions that made no sense such as "She
looked all the puppy," instead of "She liked all the puppies,"
and "She lived the little brown one" for "She loved the little
brown one." He answered four of five questions correctly
although he did not fully respond to two of the questions. As
reading this had been a difficult task for him, the examiner
reread the story to Chris and asked the last questions again.
Chris was then able to answer the missed question.

As Chris attempted to read from Level 8, it was apparent after
two lines that he could not continue. The examiner read this
part to him and asked the questions to get a listening comprehension assessment. Chris answered two of the five questions
correctly; on another question he gave one part of a two part
answer; and on another, one part of three. The questions were
restated in an attempt to elicit further responses, but none
were given. The Oral Reading Inventory ended at that point.

On a Word Recognition Inventory which is a sampling of sight
words from the Holt books, Chris was able to read 18 of the 20
words taken from Holt Levels 3-6. He read "sitter" for "sister"
and "read" for "road." On the list of 20 sample words for
Level 7 Chris was able to correctly name 10. At that time he
became very concerned with the examiner's reaction to his
answers. He looked over to see what was being written after
each of his responses. (A correct answer gets a "+" and an
incorrect word is written out for later analysis.) At one
point, the examiner wrote out a word that Chris had given
correctly, "then." When Chris noted that a word was being
written he changed his answer to "tin." Only after the word
was erased on the sheet and the question, "What do you think
it is?" was he able to answer "then." As Chris' incorrect
responses indicated some difficulty with phonics application
and possibly left to right orientation with "cop" for "pick"
and "orp" for "rope," the examiner decided to administer a
portion of the Botel Reading Inventory.

The word lists for Parts 4 and 5 on the Decoding Test of the
Botel Reading Inventory give an indication of a child's ability
to apply phonics generalizations and to recognize words with a
common spelling pattern. The 10 word list for Part 4 includes
words such as sap, yell, kiss, cob, mug with CVC (consonant-
vowel-consonant) patterns. Chris was able to name only two
from the list. These were rig and jot. It took three tries
to name jot. He said "stape" for "sap," "yawl" for "yell,"

- 4 -

Christopher Darkins, continued

"kids" for "kiss," etc. On the 10 word list for Part 5 which uses the CVCE spelling pattern in rate, Pete, vine, etc., Chris was able to name only "hope." He said "winter" for "rate," "pit" and "Peter" for "Pete," and "valentine" for "vine."

The examiner decided to end the assessment by having Chris read from one of his Ladybird books. Chris was asked to choose his favorite and read a portion of it. He did this willingly and read fluently through approximately half the book when the examiner ended the session.

Test Results and Interpretation

Chris was able to read the oral reading passages for Levels 3 through 6 and met the Holt criteria for success. On Holt Levels 3, 4, 5 and 6, Chris knew most of the vocabulary and could answer the questions about what he had read.

On Holt Level 7 he made 13 errors which affected meaning as he read the passage aloud. Even discounting errors such as "puppy" for "puppies," he still made 10 errors on the Level 7 passage. This gives a percentage correct of 80-89% for word recognition. According to the criteria established by Holt, a word recognition score of 80-89% indicates that a child is reading at his frustration level. He had a score of 80% correct on the comprehension questions for Level 7.

At Level 8 only a listening comprehension score could be obtained. His score was 57% correct on the listening comprehension questions.

On the Holt Word Recognition Inventory list for Levels 3-6, Chris was able to name 90% of the words correctly. This suggests that he knows most of the sight vocabulary for these levels. He could name 50% of the words on the Level 7 list. He was able to use beginning and ending consonant sounds on several of the words he attempted, but missed. He said "went" for "white," "fanned" for "find," "salve" for "save," "motor" for "mother." He could not apply vowel sounds on most of the words missed. He was able to use the or in "morning" as he called it "morg."

Chris' responses on the CVC word list of the Botel Reading Inventory on which he named 2 of the 10 words correctly again indicate that he was able to apply beginning and ending consonant sounds to CVC words in isolation, but did not apply short vowel sounds.

- 5 -

Christopher Darkins, continued

He attempted to apply beginning and ending sounds on most words on the CVCE word list from the Botel. He correctly named 1 word on the list of 10 words. He did not use the long vowel sound of CVCE pattern words except in his single correct response of "hope."

Christopher Darkins   February 4, 1981

Holt Placement Inventory
Oral Reading Inventory

	Word Recognition	Comprehension
Level 3	90 - 100%	100%
Level 4	90 - 100%	100%
Level 5	90 - 100%	100%
Level 6	90 - 100%	100%
Level 7	80 - 89%	80%
Level 8	Could not read passage	

Word Recognition Inventory

Levels 3-6	90%
Level 7	50%

A Name I Can't Read

Reflections

I reflected on the testing process and thought about how serious Chris was. He was ready to take all the test Mrs. Curtis gave him. Not once did I hear him complain or question Mrs. Curtis about why she asked him to read the passages to her. Somehow, I think he knew he had to do well on the tests so that he would be placed in a reading group with the rest of the children in his class. Ironically, here we were trying to prove that Chris could read so that he would be taught to read. The thought horrifies me. The reality is devastating.

It troubled me to think that if I had not taught Chris to read, he would not be able to read. He would not be able to pass the test the district had just administered to him. Then, that would be used as proof that he was not ready to read and was justly excluded from the reading groups.

If another year had passed and he did not know how to read, no one would consider that, in Kindergarten, Chris scored in the top ten percentile on the Metropolitan Readiness Test. The end of the Kindergarten year is when those scores are looked at for predicting the level at which a child should be expected to succeed. After that, a child will usually be expected to start each new level from the level just completed.

The manner in which Chris' reading exposure was curtailed at Wren Lake Elementary would have assured that he would not start reading Level 3 until Second Grade, more than a year behind his current classmates. And in order for Chris to read at a level as low as Level 3 in Second Grade, he would have to be in with a group of Kindergarten children or in "Special Education". The reality of the matter is that being in Level 2 in First Grade means that he must already be in some form of "Special Education". I tremble at the thought of how my child was robbed of a good academic start.

Because of my experience with teaching Chris to read, I can confidently say that the first readers at Level 3, 4, 5 and 6 take no more than two to four weeks for the average child to complete. As for Level 7, Mr. Palmer told us, when Gregory had reading placement difficulty at the school, that Level 7 should take about 6 weeks for the average child to complete. Given the likelihood that the majority of Chris' classmates were average or above average, some of them had probably reached Level 8 by this time. Yet Chris' teacher kept him in a picture book for over six months. More than half the school year had passed and Chris was only half way through the Level 2 picture book at school. How cruel? How criminal?

This whole ordeal had truly become a waking nightmare for me. Chris must have suffered a great loss of confidence and self-esteem watching and knowing that the teacher taught the other children in the class but did not teach him. It is hard to fathom such cruelty. As I lay awake many a night wondering how this could be happening to us again, I wondered how many other parents were experiencing this travesty. I questioned whether certain children were not being taught because of racial and ethnic prejudice. Were Blacks and other ethnic minorities who live in predominantly White school districts being targeted first for "Special Education" placement regardless of their ability to learn? I am certain that the failure to instruct a child will make him or her appear incapable of learning. How distressing!

We waited for a meeting with the district regarding their findings and recommendations.

District Findings and Recommendations

Mrs. Curtis informed us about the meeting scheduled at the school to discuss the testing results and placement for Chris. Both my husband and I went to the school for the meeting. In attendance at the meeting were the Reading Coordinator, the Supervising Reading Coordinator, the Principal, and Chris' teacher.

At the onset of the meeting, Mr. Palmer informed us that he and Mrs. Burton had already talked and made a decision. He said that although Chris was successful through level 6, they decided that Chris should be placed in Level 3. Mr. Palmer explained that there are a lot of skills taught at Level 3 other than just reading the words, and Chris needed to start at Level 3 to get those skills. We countered that even if Level 3 skills were needed, those skills could be taught while they taught Chris at the appropriate reading level as indicated by his test results.

We pressed for Chris' placement at Level 8 because we understood his test results to indicate that he successfully performed through Level 7. I related a prior conversation with Mr. Palmer about placement in Holt where he said the publisher's guidelines suggested that if a child scored 80% or above on a level placement test, he should be placed at the next higher level. Chris had scored above 80% on Level 7. Mr. Palmer quickly countered that the school did not have a First Grade group that read at Level 8. This tempted me to ask if they had any First Grade groups that read at Level 2. Instead, I asked about placing Chris in a group outside the First Grade. I already reasoned that the school would have had to place Chris outside the First Grade in order to keep him in a reading group as low as Level 2.

Mrs. Curtis feigned interest in Chris' welfare by stating that my suggested placement of Chris in Level 8 would not be good for Chris because he could not possibly have learned the skills he needed for Level 8 while in Level 2. In this tense moment, we reminded Mrs. Curtis that Chris had a tutor who could help him in areas where the school and or district felt he needed help. We all finally agreed that Chris would be placed at reading Level 6.

Mr. Palmer questioned us about whether we had a problem with Mrs. Burton teaching Chris and asked if we wanted him to move Chris to another teacher. We told him that we simply wanted Chris to be taught, and if Mrs. Burton was going to do that, we did not have a problem with Chris remaining in her class. At that point, Mrs. Burton, heavy with child, haughtily got up, walked out of the room and slammed the door behind her.

The discussion then turned to the logistics of moving Chris into Level 6. I suggested that Chris should be placed in an existing group that was progressing rapidly enough to complete Level 6 and go on to Level 7 and complete it before the end of the school year. The principal rejected my suggestion by saying they did not want to place Chris in an existing group at Level 6 because the other children had covered a lot of material in the book. He wanted to wait until they could form a small Level 6 reading group. We came to an impasse. We were discouraged because of a previous exposure to Mr. Palmer in the forming of a small reading group for our older son. Mr. Palmer formed a non-existent reading group and placed Gregory in it. A copy of a letter from Mr. Palmer about the placement decision follows.

School District U·46

Office of the Principal

` ⌐ `   ` SCHOOL

February 13, 1981

Dear Mr. & Mrs. Darkins,

This letter is to review briefly our conversation and decision on Chris last Tuesday, February 10th.

Mrs. Curtis' testing showed that Chris is ready for level six. The teacher should also make sure he has been taught the necessary skills of levels three, four and five.

Mrs. Burtch will continue with Chris in her homeroom and will begin a small reading group in level six.

We will continue to do our best in meeting the instructional goals of your son. Communication with Chris' tutor is essential. Please have the tutor call Mrs. Burtch immediately so that we can have a unified and reinforcing reading program for Chris.

If you have further questions, please call me.

Cordially yours,

cc/Mrs. `
   Mrs. `

A Cry For Help

After the meeting, I talked with Shelly about the decision for the school to place Chris at Level 6. I told her about the discussion of the skills that Chris needed and had missed while in Level 2. Shelly contacted Chris' teacher and requested information about areas where the teacher felt Chris needed help. Again, Shelly expressed that the district made skill building material available and if the school would give her the material, she would include it in Chris' tutoring sessions. Shelly went to the school for a meeting with Mrs. Burton. However, because she indicated that she did not receive information specific enough on what Chris needed help with, I wrote a letter to Mrs. Burton requesting information about areas where Chris needed help. The text of that letter follows.

A Name I Can't Read

Elgin, Illinois
March 20, 1981

Re: Student-Chris Darkins
Teacher-
Grade---1

Dear Mrs. _____,
We appreciate your taking the time to meet with Chris's tutor.
Her goal, with Chris, at this time, is to assist in any areas
where you feel his skills need additional reinforcements. However, she does not feel that she has a clear idea what problems
he is having in school.

Please let us know where Chris is at this time and how his tutor
can help by completing the enclosed form. Several forms are
enclosed for use as Chris's needs change. any reinforcement
work sheets that you can provide will help.

If you have any concerns about Chris, please let me know. Thank
you in advance.

Sincerely,

Claudia M. Darkins
Claudia M. Darkins

cc: Mr.

A Cry For Help

Student-Chris Darkins
Teacher-_____

Student's Level_____Unit_____

Check the appropriate item and complete as necessary.

O Chris does not need additional help at this time.

O Chris needs help with the following skills. (please specify)

    a.

    b.

    c.

A Name I Can't Read

Paranoia Coupled With Fear

After appealing to the school district for help in getting the school to provide the proper instruction for Gregory and Chris, I felt a great deal of hostility from the Principal and the teachers who taught our children. Our relationship with the school had deteriorated tremendously by this time. With all the talk and testing, I did not believe the school planned to teach Gregory and Chris anything about reading, writing and arithmetic. However, what became even more stressful for me was the realization I came to about what was happening. One night I awoke, startled and in a cold sweat. I realized that the school was an unhealthy environment for our children. I became fearful about my children attending Wren Lake school.

I thought, "I have made these people very angry. They do not feel responsible for teaching my children, and I should not continue to send my children to them each day."

I feared that they were damaging my children in ways I would never know. I felt traumatized and afraid. It dawned heavily on me that the school was deliberately attempting to make our children illiterate; and my efforts to get the school to teach my children made them angry. They still called me Mrs., but there was hostility in their voices and they glared at me. It dawned on me that while I went to work more than 15 miles from the school, my children went to school to angry, hostile people. We began searching for a school that would be good for our children. I was so stressed out that I considered keeping the boys out of school for the rest of the school year in order to reduce my anxiety, but I did not. I suffered tremendously for the rest of the school year. Not only was I stressed, but I believe that the headaches and stomach aches that Chris complained about were probably stress related as well.

My husband had a hard time believing that the teachers would purposely not teach our children. He was upset and frustrated that Gregory was not doing well in school and attributed the lack of success to Gregory and not to the school. He felt that it must be something that Gregory did not do that caused his teachers to send him out of the classroom for special help and lower level work. He wondered if I was obsessed and had blown things all out of proportion. However, when I pointed out Chris' situation, he had to acknowledge that there was no excuse for the school not teaching him.

Chris and Gregory finished the school year at Wren Lake Elementary, but they did not return the next Fall.

6
Rays of Hope

Gregory's dad found out about Brentwood Christian Academy through some of the people where he worked. When he told me about it, I was hopeful that it would be a place where our children could go and the teachers would teach them along with the other children. The school was located in Des Plaines, a town east of Mt. Prospect. We started the application process right away. I explained Gregory's situation giving details of the events of the last several years. The boys were accepted to start in the fall of the upcoming school year. Although most of the teachers and administrators were white, I trusted them to be fair and teach our children. I felt a great sense of relief that we had found a new place for the boys to attend school and my stress levels subsided.

The school accepted Gregory into the Fifth Grade with the understanding that he would be given extra help as needed. In addition, we signed Gregory up for the after school tutoring program. Since he would stay after school for day care, he would be at the school during that time anyway. Aside from allowing time for Gregory's tutoring, the after school program gave Chris a chance to take his first piano lessons. Since Gregory could not take piano lessons at school, I enrolled him in piano lessons at a music store in Elgin. The children's dad had enrolled them in a soccer program outside the school. Gregory did not participate in the school's soccer program because he was receiving help with his studies. Gregory was also taking swim classes at the Y and his dad expressed that we were sending the wrong message by continuing to enroll Gregory in swim classes when he could use that time to study more. I, on the other hand, felt that Gregory needed to participate in some areas of self development outside the school system. I was pleased that he expressed an interest in piano lessons and, although, the swimming lessons were not his idea, he progressed exceptionally well and enjoyed the lessons.

At first my husband worked near the school. He took the boys to school in the morning and picked them up after work. However, after the children had been in the school for a little over a month, the company where my husband worked laid him off his job. He looked all over for work in a depressed job market without success. Eventually, near the middle of the school year, he took a job in Houston, Texas.

With the children's father away, we got up very early. I drove the 17 miles to where I worked and then drove the additional miles past there to get to the school. Then I drove back to where I worked. In the evenings after work, I repeated the process. I drove about 60 additional miles each day. On a couple of occasions, during the winter, when the roads were bad due to severe weather conditions, we could not make it back to Elgin at all. We had to stay with friends who lived closer to the school. In any case, by the time I picked the children up after an early morning start, they were very tired. Slow traffic a lot of the time caused us to stop for the dinner meal on the way home; so, we got home pretty late a lot of the time. The inconvenience of getting to and from school and the expense of going there really made me feel resentful that we were not able to send our children to our neighborhood school. But what could we do? Given the circumstances, we had no other choice.

Gregory in Fifth Grade

The Fifth Grade teacher, Mrs. Hines, worked with Gregory. As expected, she said he was below grade level in reading and needed a tutor for a number of language skills. However, after working with him, she expressed that he had the ability to do the work and showed a desire to learn. I felt encouraged.

On one occasion, Gregory said to me, "Mommy, I wish you had found this school for me before. Mrs. Hines is teaching me in class with everyone else."

Gregory was proud to be going to the Brentwood Baptist Christian Academy. I was glad because of the tutoring Gregory received and because of the good feelings he seemed to develop about himself and his own abilities. Plus, I was glad that he was excited about going to school.

Gregory's grades were terrible while he was at the Academy. However, Mrs. Hines always had a good report about his progress. She said he wanted to learn and was catching on and learning very well.

At the end of the school year. Mrs. Hines asked to meet with me regarding Gregory's progress. I met with both Mrs. Hines and the dean of the school. Mrs. Hines said Gregory improved tremendously during the school year. However, she felt that he should repeat the Fifth Grade. She believed he had improved to the point where he would be able to work on his own in the Fifth Grade the next year.

I reminded Mrs. Hines and the dean that Gregory would not be returning to the Academy the next year because we planned to move to the greater Houston area as soon as school ended and we were able to sell our house in Elgin. Mrs. Hines gave us the name of a Christian school in the Houston area. She suggested that we register the children at Westbury Christian Academy in Houston.

Chris in Second Grade

Chris went into the Second Grade at the Brentwood Christian Academy. Miss Loucas was his teacher. Shortly, after the school year started, Chris' stomach aches began again. His father took him to the doctor and they admitted him into the hospital in an effort to determine the source of his problem. Chris spent a week in the hospital, but the doctors did not determine the cause of his problem.

Chris missed that whole week of school and before he went back, I had a conference with Miss Loucas. During the conference, I asked to see Chris' reading book which the children were not allowed to bring home. After reviewing the book, I explained to Miss Loucas that the reading level of the book was much too low for Chris. I asked Miss Loucas why she placed Chris at such a low level. She explained that the school had a policy of automatically placing children who transferred from the public schools at a lower reading level than their regular students because the transferring students usually performed at a lower level.

I began to feel disillusionment about this new school and their ability to treat my children fairly, but I felt they should be given the benefit of the doubt: this was probably a systematic bias as Miss Loucas explained. I, calmly, asked Miss Loucas to have an assessment made to determine Chris' proper reading placement. Not only did I feel this low reading level placement would be a source of frustration and stress for him; I also wanted him to be placed properly.

The school made the assessment and Chris' teacher raised his reading level. Knock on wood, Chris stopped complaining about the stomach aches for the duration of the school year. To my delight, he made the honor roll at the end of one of the subsequent six week reporting periods.

The children continued to attend Brentwood Christian Academy until the end of the school year. We planned to join my husband in Houston as arrangements could be made to sell our house. However, the glut of vacant houses on the market made our house very difficult to sell. A lot of people had been laid off from their jobs, and because of the scarcity of jobs in the area, they either lost or left their homes and moved to the site of their new jobs. A vacant house stood across the street from ours. The couple who lived there had remodeled just before moving. They listed it for a lower price than we were asking for ours. The owners of a house just like ours, across the main street, in the facing cul-de-sac, listed their house for a price less than ours. Our first real estate broker had so many houses that he didn't even put a "for sale" sign in front of ours. I changed brokers. The enthusiastic new broker took pictures and placed a "for sale" sign in the yard.

We could see how long houses were staying on the market, so I told everyone I knew or met that our house was up for sale and asked if they wanted to buy it. Then, one day a couple came to our garage sale. The parents of the women lived in the same cul-de-sac as we did, and they sometimes baby sat their two grandchildren. I asked the couple if they were interested in buying a house near the grandparents and showed them around the house. The wife said they called their realtor about our house as soon as they saw the "for sale" sign go up, but their realtor did not show it to them because he felt they could not afford it at the time. I asked if they might be interested in leasing it with the option to buy in a years time. They called their realtor and leased the house with the option to buy. Fortunately, at the end of the year, they bought the house.

7
The Cycle Continues

At the end of July 1982, we moved to Minter City, a suburb of Houston, Texas. Shortly after we arrived in the Houston area, I went to Westbury Christian Academy to see about getting Gregory and Chris admitted. When I talked to a school administrator, he told me about two requirements for admittance to the school. First, that the child be doing well at the school where he last attended. Secondly, they required that the child be at grade level. I did not expect this since Brentwood Christian Academy recommended the school to us.

We enrolled the children in John Smith Elementary, the public school which served the area where we bought a house. The school was situated in one of the older subdivisions of Minter City. Most of the students, teachers and administrators at the school were white at that time. The areas surrounding the school were predominantly white, but changed rapidly as more Blacks bought homes in the area and Whites moved out. Also, the faltering job market caused a lot of families to leave the area in search of new jobs.

When I enrolled the children, I talked to Mrs. Sanchez, the Principal. I asked her how the school did reading and math placement for children who came from other schools. She said the children would be given a placement test to determine where they should be placed, and then the school would place them accordingly.

Mrs. Sanchez showed us around the school. The open classroom concept had been implemented in the school for the Fifth Grade. The Fifth Grade classrooms had no walls except for the ones that enclosed the large area where the classes were. A set of bookshelves divided the classes. The bookshelves stood about three feet high. The children in one class could easily look over into another without a problem. It was hard to imagine how teachers maintained order when one class decided to play a game or have a competition and another class wanted to be involved in quiet class work.

Gregory Repeats the Fifth Grade

Shortly after school started, I checked with the school to see how Gregory did on the placement tests. I was pleased and relieved that Gregory had done well enough to be taught at Fifth Grade level. I talked to Gregory's math and reading teachers and requested that they contact me if Gregory appeared to have problems with his school work. I wanted to know at the earliest possible point so that I could start seeking help if it became necessary.

Right away, I started asking Gregory to show me some of his work. He told me his teachers kept his work in folders in the classroom. I asked to see his math book. (I understood that he would not be allowed to bring the reading book home.) Gregory told me they were not allowed to bring the math book home either. He further explained that he did not have a math book of his own and had to use someone else's book every day. I did not fully understand the meaning of his statement, but I made an appointment with his math teacher to get an understanding of the math book question.

Before my appointment with his math teacher, Gregory brought home a slip from his math teacher requesting payment for a lost math book. I asked Gregory how he lost his math book.

He said his teacher did not give him a math book. He said she told him that if he wanted a math book, he would have to pay for one and gave him the slip to bring home. I told him I would have to talk to his teacher before buying a book because he had never brought the book home.

Gregory's teacher and I discussed the lost math book issue. I explained that Gregory never brought a math book home and could not possibly have lost it there. I asked her if the school had a lost and found that could be checked in case the book had been left on the bus, on a table in the hall, on the grounds or elsewhere. She said she'd checked the lost and found before sending the notice and the book wasn't there. On a chance that it might have turned up since then, I wanted to check it again. I checked, but I did not find a math book in the lost and found.

I asked if she minded my looking through his desk and around the room in general. She said she had already checked, and the book was not found there. I asked if he had a locker where he might keep the book after leaving the classroom to go to other activities. She explained that the children were not allowed to take the math books from the classroom. She collected the books before the children left the classroom.

"Oh", I observed, "If he never leaves the classroom with the book; how can he lose it? Where do you keep the books?", I asked hopeful.

She pointed to a bookshelf with the math books for the class stacked on it. She passed the books out each day at the beginning of class, collected them from the children at the end of the class and returned them to the shelf.

"How do you know that one of the books on the shelf does not belong to Gregory?" I wanted to know.

The teacher explained that each book has a number stamped in it, and none of the books on the shelf had the number of the book she assigned to Gregory.

I asked the teacher how she could justify holding Gregory responsible for a book that she had never allowed him to take from the classroom. She responded that once a child is issued a book and that book is lost, she cannot issue another book until the parent pays for the lost book.

"So, does that mean Gregory has not had a book to work from since his book was lost?", I asked.

"Oh no, there are almost always extra books on the shelf, and if there isn't one, he can use my book.", she replied.

"What if you're using your book?", I asked.

She said that if she was, she would let him use one of the other books at her desk. She had other books at her desk that she couldn't issue in place of a lost book until it had been paid for.

My primary concern became that Gregory have a book so that he could do his work and not became idle. If he did not have a book to do his work, his skill development would suffer. His teacher assured me that Gregory would not have a problem getting a book to use in class. Considering that the children were not allowed to take the books out of the classroom and considering that Gregory's teacher said he would have a book to do his class work, I told his teacher that I would wait to see if the book turned up rather than immediately paying for it. I suggested that the next book could be lost just as mysteriously. Plus, I had not yet landed a job in the Houston area and did not want to take on the expense of a book unless it was absolutely necessary.

We finished the discussion about the lost book and I asked about Gregory's performance on math assignments and homework. His teacher informed me that she did not give homework and that all assignments had to be completed in the classroom during the time allowed. She said that the students had plenty of time to do their work during the block of time they had in her classroom.

As the school year progressed, I had several conferences with Gregory's math teacher. During several of those conferences she pointed out Gregory's inability to complete his class work during the time allotted.

The Cycle Continues

I asked if a book was always available for him to do his work and the teacher reassured me that a book was always available. She said she did not understand why he could not finish the work. On the positive side, the teacher commented that the work Gregory actually did showed his ability to master the work and she stated that his behavior was good. Because they were not allowed to bring the math books home, I gave the teacher several stamped postcards addressed to me. I asked her to send me the postcards to keep me informed about what they were covering in order for me to help Gregory at home. I did not receive any of the postcards back.

Book Theft Accusation

Very late in the school year, I bumped into one of the other fifth grade teachers in front of the grocery store. This teacher's classroom was located in the same open area as Gregory's math class. She asked if the school had contacted me about the book problem. She told me that Gregory's math teacher had very loudly accused him of stealing a book. She figured I had been called or sent a note. I told her that I had not received a call or a note and that Gregory had not mentioned it to me. I knew nothing about it. She said she was surprised I had not been notified by the school.

With that information, I went home and discussed the matter with Gregory. He explained that his teacher accused him of stealing a math book because he wrote his name in the math book that she let him use. He told me that after the teacher gave the other children their books, she gave him a book to use. He put his name in the book so the teacher would call his name along with the other children, and he would not have to wait as long for the teacher to give him a book. He told me the teacher did not always give him a book right away. Sometimes, he had to wait while she did some other things or until she knew that no other children were coming to class.

107

A Name I Can't Read

I asked him about whether he had written his name in the math book given to him at the beginning of the school year. He said his teacher did not issue him a book at the beginning of the school year. He explained that when she started issuing the books, she sent him out of the classroom for testing. When he returned on a different day, a substitute teacher was in charge of the class. The substitute gave him a book to use during class time, but collected it when class was over. He told the substitute he had not been issued a book, but the substitute told him that she could not issue books. When the teacher returned, he asked her for a book, but she told him that he would have to pay for a book before she would issue one to him.

After listening to Gregory's understanding, I went to the school to speak with his math teacher. I let her know that I had been told about her accusing Gregory of stealing a math book. I explained that in talking with Gregory, he understood that she had not issued him a book at the beginning of the school year. Because she did not issue him a book, in desperation, he wrote his name in a book hoping that would cause her to give him a book at the beginning of class along with the other children the next time she distributed the books. He wanted to start on his work right away. She looked at me until I finished my statement before she spoke.

She said she had cleared up the problem and that she had already apologized to Gregory. She said it was her mistake for not issuing Gregory a book. However, she went on to say her mistake of not issuing Gregory a book was still no excuse for him to write his name in a book that did not belong to him.

I could no longer remain calm and collected. I felt myself becoming even more agitated than when I first heard about her accusation against my child. I told her that she needed to admit that she was the cause of this problem. A simple check of her record book would have reminded her that she had not issued Gregory a math book long before now. I let her know that it was difficult for me to understand how she could send a notice to me asking payment for the book without first checking her record book. How could she know what book to look for on the shelf or in the lost and found if she didn't check her record book for a book number? Checking the record book would have alerted her that she had not issued Gregory a book if she did not already know it.

At this point, no question existed in my mind that her failure to issue Gregory a math book was purposeful and intended to prevent him from completing his work during the time allowed. I told her that when she complained that he was not finishing his work on time, she knew she was not giving him a math book right away. Even if she thought she issued him a book, that was no excuse for making him wait to get a book each day. She could have given him one of the books at her desk and not waited to see which children might come late before giving him a book to use. I told her that it was difficult for me to believe she had not done this purposely to keep Gregory from making the grade. She knew the importance of starting right away on class work. She gazed at me while I spoke. When I finished, she just shrugged her shoulders and repeated that she had already apologized to Gregory. Since she seemed to think that her apology justified her behavior, I told her that there is a big difference between loudly accusing a child of stealing in front of all the classes in the open area and then apologizing to him in private.

I felt extremely distressed after meeting with Gregory's teacher. No explanation seemed reasonable for me to understand how the failure to issue the math book was a mistake. The teacher's behavior appeared to be a means of preventing my child from getting his assignments done on time. She exercised control over the books and Gregory was helpless to determine when he would get a book.

It became evident that we were going through the same old problems again at this school. With the end of the school year in sight, there was not much I could do to undo the damage that had already happened. Why had she done this to my child? As sad as it may seem, I figured she could not pass up the opportunity to victimize this Black child.

The classroom instruction and special help Gregory received during the year at the academy and the tutoring he received the year before helped him progress to the brink of recovering from the early years when he was excluded from the teaching/learning process. His test scores at the beginning of the school year allowed him to be placed in a regular Fifth Grade math class. Now, this effort to prevent his math skill development became still another damaging blow to his progress. Although, this occurrence disheartened me, I think Gregory felt defeated throughout the school year. Imagine, wanting to do your work and being denied a book.

Even with all of this negative activity, one positive area for Gregory that year was in his art class. Gregory's art teacher expressed that he had a real talent for art. At the art showing for the class, near the end of the school year, Gregory made sure I got to see his art work. It was a source of pride for him. His enthusiasm moved me so much that I wanted him to take Art in junior high school rather than music. But, he liked music and wanted to learn more about it. He signed up to take music appreciation during the next year in middle school.

This marked the end of Gregory's years in elementary school. The next year he went on to Minter City Junior High School.

Chris in Third Grade

Chris went into Third Grade at John Smith Elementary. A few weeks after school started, Chris brought home a note requesting payment for a book. The note indicated that he could not be issued another book until he paid for the lost book. The book was expensive; especially considering that I did not even have a job yet. At the same time Chris brought home another note saying that he did not always do his work. Chris was anxious for me to take care of the book situation because he said he did not have a book to use for his class work assignments. He said that he had to borrow a book from one of the other children after the other child finished his work.

I promptly, made an appointment to talk to Chris' teacher. I wanted to discuss his failure to do his work with her. Chris had a reputation from his previous school, the tutor and from me of always doing his work promptly and consistently. I wanted to understand the problem so that it could be corrected right away.

Before going to the school, I quizzed Chris about the lost book. He explained that when the teacher issued the books, she said she had run out of books and told him to share the book she issued the child who sat next to him. Sometime later, the school nurse sent Chris home with a headache and a nosebleed. When he returned to school, the other child had a different seat assignment and Chris had no book to use for his work. When he asked the teacher for a book, she told him he would have to buy a book. She gave him the book payment notice when he told her she needed to tell his parents how much the book cost so they could send the money.

As soon as I got to the school for the conference, I related this story about the lost book not being issued to Chris. I wanted to get that issue out of the way. The teacher checked her record book and agreed that she had not issued Chris a book.

"Don't you check your record book before you send out notices for parents to pay for books?", I asked.

"These books are not cheap, and I'd hate to pay for a book that was not issued to Chris.", I pointed out.

"Well, you get the money back at the end of the school year when the book turns up.", the teacher shrugged.

"But there is no book to turn up.", I thought, but did not say it because I did not want to belabor the point.

The teacher went on to say she normally checked, but since she thought she issued the book, she did not bother to check this time.

Having cleared that up, we went on to talk about the work she said Chris did not finish. The work was from the book she did not issue to Chris, so I told her she needed to give him a chance to do the work after she issued him the book. I explained that, as a rule, Chris does his work promptly, and her note greatly concerned me. I wanted to make sure his good work habits did not change.

Chris' teacher went on to tell me she had concerns about his ability to do the language work assignments. She said that she had a habit of saving a file of some of the children's work, so that she would have it to show when parents came in with concerns. The children's work is sent home in a folder, but she was holding some of the work out as proof of a problem.

"How do we know about the problem, if you don't send the problem papers home?", I asked.

"I tell the parents when they come in for a conference.", she said as she took some of Chris' papers out of a folder.

"These papers indicate Chris' lack of ability.", she continued.

I looked at the papers. Then, I took a closer look at some of the answers that were marked as incorrect. As I looked at one of the questions, I pointed out to her that Chris' answer was the only possible answer, of those given, for the question.

"You can't fill in this blank with any of these other choices.", I told her.

"Maybe you should regrade this.", I suggested.

As a result of our exchange, I became discouraged by her desire to show Chris incapable of learning and I silently questioned her ability to effectively teach children.

After that I let Chris' teacher know that another reason I wanted to have a conference with her was so I could see Chris' reading book since they were not allowed to bring the books home. She showed me the book. The book was way below the difficulty level that I expected Chris to be reading at.

I asked, "What grade is this book for? Is this a Third Grade book?"

She explained that it was a Second Grade book used for a blended group of children at different grades levels. I asked why Chris was placed at that level because the reading level was much too low for him. She said that she had nothing to do with placement. The lead teacher made all placements decisions. I left her and waited for a chance to talk with the lead teacher.

Mrs. Sanchez, the Principal, advised me that the lead teacher would not be available to speak with me and asked if she could help. I explained the reading level problem to Mrs. Sanchez. I reminded her of our discussion during the summer, when she told me that new students were placed in Reading and Math based on placement test they would be given. She acknowledged the process I stated as the placement procedure. I explained that because Chris normally tested well above his grade level, I could not understand why he was placed below grade level in Reading. I asked to see his test results. Mrs. Sanchez told me she would have to talk to the lead teacher. I waited while she went to find out about the test. When she returned, she told me the test could not be located. She assured me that Chris would be retested and placed accordingly. After the testing, the school placed Chris under a different teacher altogether.

Gregory in Middle School

Gregory's academic situation did not improve much in middle school. He just got older. During the first year Gregory took music appreciation and did poorly. His teacher, a young woman who was perhaps in her first year as a teacher, was very negative in her criticism of Gregory; however, her comments were so vague and generalized that I did not really understand the problem or how to effectively help him. I actually felt that she was the problem.

The second year Gregory took a band class and the results were phenomenal. Gregory learned to read music and play the trombone. Mr. Munson, the Band Director, made it a point to tell us that Gregory had a special talent in music. Gregory usually made first chair, and Mr. Munson recommended him for tutoring by professional musicians who came to the school to tutor students who showed promise.

After one conference where Mr. Munson praised Gregory in Music, we had a conference with Gregory's language teacher. She told us Gregory was doing poorly in her class. She did not give us a clear understanding of what his problems were in Language, but she told us he was probably doing poorly in Music as well because the two go hand in hand. She said that when a child does poorly in one, you will find that he does poorly in the other.

"Well", I proudly informed her, "I have just had a conference with Mr. Munson, and Gregory is doing great in Music; he can read music and he takes first chair."

Gregory was in the seventh grade then, but I still remember how good it felt for Gregory's performance in music to disprove her idea that he was not doing well in music because he was not doing well in her class. Gregory continued to do well in Music and at the end of the next school year, when it was time for him to go to high school, Mr. Munson recommended him for the highly competitive band at Eagle High School.

Chris in Fourth Grade

During Chris' first year at John Smith Elementary, the children moved from classroom to classroom. However, when Chris went to the Fourth Grade, they had made a change to keep the children in a home classroom. They went out to special classrooms for Art, Music, and subjects of that nature. However, for the core classes, the children had a main teacher and a main classroom. Mrs. Yorba was Chris' art teacher. She always had a lot of praise for his ability in art. He won a blue ribbon at the Rodeo Art Fair for one of his drawings.

By this time Chris loved to read books on his own. He signed up for a read-a-thon. He read books so rapidly that I questioned him on the content of the books before he returned them to the library. However, something else happened. I don't know what it was, but Chris lost his enthusiasm for checking out and reading so many books on his own.

Chris started having stomach aches and headaches again. Also, he started having profuse nosebleeds more often than I care to think about. Periodically, the school called us to get Chris from school because they could not stop his nosebleed. When this happened, we picked him up from school. When he went back to school, I sent a note explaining that he had been sent home by the school nurse and requesting that he be given a chance to do all the work assignments he missed while he was out.

When I went for conferences, Chris' teacher always seemed to have some vague generalized complaints about Chris or his work. However, she never specifically explained the problems so that I could adequately address them. One evening at a conference, she showed me some zeroes in her grade book for him. (The zeroes really hurt his grade because a zero and two 100's when averaged comes to 66, which was an F.) I asked what he did to cause him to miss the work, but she just shrugged. I told her that I would talk to Chris to make sure he understood how badly zeroes hurt his grade and how important it is for him to do all of his work.

After that I asked if Chris had made up all the work he missed on the days he was sent home by the nurse. The Teacher shrugged her shoulders and said she wasn't sure. I told her that I was anxious to know because I didn't want that work to become zeroes in the grade book. I had the dates of his absences with me and asked her to check her grade book for those days. She still had the grade book open and I noticed that the zeroes were for days he was sent home. I pointed this out to the teacher. She said it was Chris' responsibility to make sure he got all of the assignments, and if he did not he would get zeroes for it.

"No that can't be his responsibility!", I countered.

115

"Chris has no way of knowing what work he misses when he is out. It's your responsibility to give him the work. His responsibility is to do the work that you give him."

I reminded her that I sent notes requesting that Chris be given a chance to make up the work he missed while he was out. I understood that this was all I had to do in order for him to be given the work. Also, I explained that Chris told me he had asked her for the work he missed, but he didn't know if she gave him all of the work or not. I told her that Chris' concern about this was the reason I had the makeup work on my list of things to check with her about. I explained to her that it was not fair for her to turn Chris' A's into F's because of work she did not give him a chance to do. I suggested that it would be fine for her to send the work home with me, but she said she would have to find time to give him the work. I sensed that this teacher had a negative attitude toward Chris and that there was not much I could do about it. I looked forward to Chris getting out of her class.

At the end of one of the six week grading periods, Chris got a bad grade in history. Since the school offered tutoring on campus, I decided to send Chris to the school's tutoring program. Tutoring was offered in the mornings before school started. If children waited to ride the bus, they would not get to school in time for tutoring. So, I drove Chris to school early for tutoring. During the first week, I went in and gave the tutor my phone number and asked her to let me know if there were any problems. As it turned out, Chris' tutor was the math teacher Gregory had the one year he attended John Smith Elementary.

A few weeks later, I called and asked the tutor about Chris' progress. She told me Chris had done absolutely nothing since she started tutoring him.

"What does he do?", I asked.

"He does absolutely nothing.", she told me.

"Well, what is the problem, does he know what he is supposed to do? Is he being disruptive? Is he sleeping or what?", I asked.

The Cycle Continues

"I put all the work he is supposed to do in his folder, he knows what he is supposed to do, but he does absolutely nothing.", she told me.

"Is there some reason why you haven't called or sent me a note about this?", I asked. "A lot of time has gone by. I could have talked to him when the problem first started, but I'll talk to him about it when I get home.", I told her.

That evening I talked to Chris. I asked him why he would go to school for tutoring and then not do the work. I asked him to tell me what his problem was.

"Why haven't you been doing the work?", I asked.

"She's not giving me any work to help me improve my grade.", he said. "She put all the papers in my folder from tests I didn't answer all the questions on since the beginning of school. How is that going to help me now? I won't be tested on that work anymore. I tried to tell her that, but she won't talk to me. So, while I'm in there, I study for the history we are covering right now."

I didn't take Chris to school for tutoring after that.

8
Low Expectations

During the summer, after Chris's Fourth Grade school year, there was an article in the paper about House Bill 72. House Bill 72 mandated that children be placed in basic, academic or advanced level classes based on their test scores on the Iowa Test of Basic Skills. The only other way children were to be placed was by teacher recommendation.

About a week before school started, we received the results of Chris' test. We didn't know what the scores meant in relationship to placement, so I called the school district to find out. The lady who answered the phone told me that parents did not need to worry about that; the schools would take care of it. Finally, as I persisted in wanting to know what the general guidelines were for placement at the different levels, she told me that the school counselor would be the one to provide that information.

I called the school and asked the school counselor to give me the score breakdown for placement at the various levels. I told her I had the test results, but I didn't know where my child should be placed based on his test scores. The counselor said they were swamped with telephone inquiries about House Bill 72. For that reason, they were going to have a meeting to discuss the impact of House Bill 72 with everyone at the same time.

Several weeks of school went by before the school had the meeting. Parents packed the meeting room wanting to know about the impact of House Bill 72 on their children.

The speaker told us children would be placed according to test scores. She passed out a yellow booklet with a microscope on the cover and said that most of the questions we had would be answered by reading the booklet. I took the booklet home and read it from cover to cover. However, it did not answer the question about what the scores meant in terms of placement levels. I still wanted to know.

I went back to the school to talk to Mrs. Sans, the school counselor. I explained that I attended the meeting called to explain the effects of House Bill 72 as it related to the placement of children. I told her that I read the little yellow booklet, and I still did not know what scores indicated that a child should be placed in basic, academic or advanced levels of study.

I had Chris' test results with me, and Mrs. Sans had Chris' folder in front of her. She told me that Chris' scores indicated placement in the advanced level for math and science and in the academic level for the language arts.

Given that information, I asked at what level the school placed Chris. She said the school had placed him at the academic level for both language arts and math and sciences.

I asked why Chris' test scores were not used to place him at the advanced level for math and science. Mrs. Sans opened up Chris' record and took out a plain sheet of paper with a small box drawn on it. Inside the box were some words and a signature.

The words were: "I recommend that Chris Darkins be placed at the academic level."

Chris' Fourth Grade teacher from the prior year had signed it. I turned the paper over and found nothing on the other side and nothing attached.

I asked, "Is this it? Does this mean that Chris was placed at the academic level in math and science based on teacher recommendation?"

Low Expectations

Mrs. Sans acknowledged "teacher recommendation" as the reason the school placed Chris at the academic level in math and science. I asked what reason the teacher gave for the recommendation. Mrs. Sans said the teacher did not give her a reason. She asked if I wanted to talk to the teacher about it. I told Mrs. Sans that I did not want to talk to the teacher because I did not think she had Chris' best interest at heart. I told her that I'd talked to the teacher several times while Chris was in her class and that I waited for him to get out of the Fourth Grade because I sensed that this teacher had a negative attitude toward him. She did not call us to discuss her intent to keep Chris from being taught at the advanced level in math and science, although his test scores indicated his ability to learn at that level. Instead, she used "teacher recommendation" as a loophole to prevent Chris from being taught at the advanced level. I told Mrs. Sans that the legislature did not intend for teacher recommendation to be used in this way because it was not in the spirit of recommendation. Recommendation is a positive term, and this teacher had used the power of recommendation negatively. I went on to say that Chris' test scores were his recommendation, and I wanted him placed according to his test scores in accordance with House Bill 72.

At that point, Mrs. Sans told me the advanced level classes were full. I told her I felt it unlikely that so many children scored at the advanced level, especially when the school had honors classes also. I wanted to see the test scores of the children in the class. I suggested that those not scoring well enough to be in the advanced level class should be placed at the academic level instead of my child being displaced. She said she could not show me the confidential scores. I told her I did not want to see names, I just wanted to see test scores. I told her that if the legislature intended House Bill 72 to cause children to be taught according to their ability as measured by the test scores, the school administrators used "teacher recommendation" to make House Bill 72 meaningless. (I noticed that the paper had been duplicated and I wondered how many children had been placed by teacher recommendation instead of by their test scores.)

Mrs. Sans told me that they would work out a plan to move Chris and get back to me in the next day or two. Already nearing the end of the first six week grading period, we agreed that Chris needed to be in the new class by the time the next six week grading period started.

After our meeting, Mrs. Sans called and asked how I wanted Chris placed in the language arts. I told her that I did not know the in and out of how they placed children, so I would have to rely upon them to place him properly. She said his test scores in the language arts showed that he should be placed at a higher level than the teacher recommended. They would go ahead and move him up, but he would still be in academic level classes for the language arts. She said he would go into the new classes at the beginning of the second six week grading period.

Unlike the previous year when the children spent the full day in the same classroom, this year the children spent half of the day in the same classroom for language arts and half of the day in another classroom for math and science. These two subject areas had a specific teacher. As soon as Mrs. Sans let me know the names of Chris' new teachers, I made an appointment for a conference with them.

First, I talked to Chris' new math and science teacher. Mr. Marsdale, a young, slender, Black man, seemed a bit annoyed because Chris was placed in his class. He asked me if I thought I knew better than Chris' teacher where he should be placed. He said that we would see what Chris could do. I told him that Chris' test scores indicated that he could be taught at the advanced level and I felt that if he did not start being taught at that level, his scores would start to go down as they already had in the language arts. I suspected that Mr. Marsdale talked to Chris' previous teacher and became biased because of it.

After that meeting, I talked to Chris' new language arts teacher. I asked her to let me know if Chris had problems in her class. She said she would, because Chris had been moved up quite a bit in academics to get from where he was to her class.

After a few weeks, Mr. Marsdale sent a progress report. He indicated that Chris had not done all of his science work. I made an appointment to discuss the problem. When I arrived for the appointment, Mr. Marsdale showed me all of the candy he took from Chris. Chris, apparently, had used his lunch money to buy candy at the store and then sold it to his school mates for a profit. The school did not have a candy machine. I told Mr. Marsdale that I didn't think Chris would bring anymore candy to the classroom now that he knew it would be taken away from him.

Then he told me about the assignments Chris had not done. The assignments had to do with a term paper for the science project. Chris had not turned in a title for his project and a preliminary outline was due. It surprised me to hear that Chris had not done his work.

"Why hasn't Chris done his work? I mean, does he know he is suppose to do this?", I asked.

I told Mr. Marsdale that I didn't understand because Chris always did his work.

"Are you sure you told him to do this?", I asked again.

"Yes, I told all the children and the rest of them have turned it in.", he told me.

I had a hard time believing the teacher gave Chris an assignment, and he simply did not do it. I asked for a copy of the assignment and told Mr. Marsdale that I would talk to Chris about why he had not done the work.

When I got home, I got on Chris' case. I showed him a copy of the assignment. He claimed he had not seen it before and knew nothing about it.

That evening and over the weekend we went out looking for extra books for Chris to use to select a science project so he could come up with a title and do an outline for his term paper. I bought an old science book for him to use. After Chris selected his project, I told him to do his outline so he could turn it in along with the title.

Chris said, "Mom, I need help. I don't know how to do an outline. The teacher hasn't taught me how to do outlines yet."

This confused me because I knew that if his teacher required him to turn in an outline, the teacher had taught him how to do it. I showed Chris how I did outlines; however, I cautioned him: "This may not be the way your teacher wants you to do it." He did the outline.

All the while, I was puzzled about why Chris didn't do the work when the teacher told him to. I wondered what was happening to Chris. How could he be in the classroom and not know the assignments and not know how to do them? I could not understand why he would claim to know nothing of the assignment? But, why would Mr. Marsdale say he gave the assignments, if he did not? This puzzled me.

I went back to the school to talk to Mr. Marsdale. I told him about my talk with Chris and how he claimed to know nothing about the assignments and said he had not been taught how to do the outline for the term paper. I explained to Mr. Marsdale that I was confused because this was unlike Chris; he usually attacked his schoolwork with zeal. I asked Mr. Marsdale if he knew of any explanation for this. He said he did not, but advised me that the term paper assignments accounted for a big part of Chris' science grade.

My confusion continued. Many weeks went by and the pattern repeated itself. Mr. Marsdale claimed to give assignments and Chris claimed to know nothing about them. I was baffled and feared we were losing Chris academically.

One day near the beginning of the last six weeks of school, I stayed home from work sick with the flu. Chris came in from school very agitated. He rushed over to my bed.

He said, "Mom, Mr. Marsdale says the absolute deadline for the finished term paper is next week, and I don't know what to do. I don't know how to do the term paper."

Low Expectations

I sighed and looked at Chris suspiciously. I thought, "How could he not know how to do the term paper? Haven't they been spending some time each week on this in science class?"

I said, "Calm down." I told him to take out the old science book, his outline and the notes he had written for his project. I told him to use his outline and write in the information about what he had done. He worked at his term paper and when he finished writing it, he typed it and took it to school to turn it in.

I was still confused about his failure in knowing about the assignments. I could see in the beginning not knowing the routine after coming to the class six weeks after school started, but I could not understand this same problem near the end of the school year. I didn't know what to think.

Finally, the night of the science fair arrived. I went around to look at all of the projects on display. I noticed Chris' project. His term paper got a grade of C+. When I left the science project area, I went to the area where Chris' language arts teacher held her conferences. I sat down to wait my turn. As she finished her conference with the parent before me, the teacher commented that most of the children seemed to be having spring fever now.

I laughed and said, "Well Chris seems to have been having some kind of fever all year long, especially in science."

Chris' language arts teacher asked what I meant, and I told her that all year Chris claimed to know nothing about the various assignments for his science project term paper. I related to her how he'd come home a few weeks before all agitated because Mr. Marsdale told them about the final deadline for the science project term paper. I told her how he claimed he didn't know anything about the deadline or how to do the term paper. I told her that I just didn't have a clue in figuring out his problem or what to do about it. Chris' language arts teacher looked at me, her eyes widened, she raised her hands and let them drop as if she had just realized something obvious.

"Why, I know what the problem is!", she exclaimed.

"You do?", I asked anxiously.

She explained, "The problem is that Chris is in my english class. They do the term papers assignments for the science project in that english class over there."

She continued to explain that a few weeks before, she noticed Mr. Marsdale go over to the other english class to talk to the children who were also in his science class. She said that because she knew Chris was in Mr. Marsdale's science class, she told Chris to go over to the other english classroom to hear what Mr. Marsdale had to say.

She looked at me for a moment and said that would explain why he did not know about the term paper assignments and had no instruction on how to go about doing it. That, also, explained why he came home agitated about the deadline for the term paper a week before it was due.

I breathed a sigh of relief because I finally understood the problem. I found relief in knowing that Chris did not willfully fail to do his work assignments and then deny knowing about them. (As I write this, I wonder who graded that science project term paper. Did Mr. Marsdale or the other english teacher?)

I thought, "What a horrible position to be in. Assigned to a class that basis a large percentage of your grade on what you do in another class, but you're not in that other class, you don't know the assignments, their due dates and you have no instruction about how to do the assignments." I felt drained. I did not go back to talk to Mr. Marsdale when I ended my conference with the english teacher. Exhausted, I went home.

The next school day, I called the counseling office to talk to Mrs. Sans about what had happened. I asked Mrs. Sans why they placed Chris in a class which was dependent on another class, and then failed to put him in the class it depended on. I asked her if she had any idea what confusion this situation caused Chris and us. Mrs. Sans remained very quiet, and I could hear the silence.

Finally, Mrs. Sans said, "We tried to place your son according to his test scores."

Low Expectations

Perhaps, she blamed me for requesting that Chris be placed according to his test scores instead of by the "teacher recommendation" that we were not informed about.

I will always remember that year because of the confusion it caused between Chris and me. I was on Chris' case at every turn when he claimed not to know about some work he had not done. Even when I helped him with the outline and with the term paper, I looked at him out of the side of my eye; I wondered whether he was trying to get out of doing his work. At times, he would cry while trying to convince me that he really didn't know about an assignment. That year was another real nightmare for me.

During this time Chris played club soccer. Several of the children who played soccer with him went to John Smith Elementary also. Most of the soccer players were White. One of the boys was in the honors classes. Two others were in the advanced math and science class with Chris. Another one had been in advanced classes, but his grandmother told me she eventually pulled him out because of the difficulty he had in doing the work and the stress it placed on her.

She said the advanced or "Super Kid" class (as it was commonly referred to) started when her grandson was in Kindergarten in anticipation of a state rule to place children according to test scores. She said her grandson didn't score well enough to be in the advanced class, but the teacher talked to her and wanted to keep him in the class. She said the teacher felt they could give him enough supportive help for him to do okay.

I do not know how the other two boys scored on the test. However, one of the parents said that the "Super Kid" program was the only reason they stayed in the district instead of moving to another area where they had already found a house. They moved to their new home, in another school district, as soon as their son graduated from the "Super Kid" program at John Smith Elementary. One other child was not doing well in the advanced math and science class; However, I don't know if it was because of ability or if he just was not doing the work. His family moved out of the district as soon as he finished Fifth Grade.

Chris Starts Junior High School

The next year, Chris entered Minter City Junior High School. By this time the majority of the children who attended the school were Black, yet most of the teachers and administrators were White. They did not identify positively with the children.

The school suffered from an extreme state of unrest, and the atmosphere at the school was very oppressive and restrictive. Parents' meetings were closed sessions. When I wanted to attend the parents' meeting, the Principal told me that the meetings were open only to selected parents who would represent the rest of the parents. However, the Principal would not give out the names or phone numbers of the selected parents because that was confidential.

I questioned him by asking, "How do they represent me if I don't know who they are?"

He gave no answer, except a smug look.

Several parents worked diligently to change the closed parents' meetings and other unhealthy school policies. In the meantime, the students rebelled. As with any unorganized upheaval, the situation had negative effects on the students, the school, the community, and race relations. The atmosphere at the school deteriorated and remained strained for a long season.

This upheaval occurred near the end of Chris's first year at Minter City Junior High School. A number of the parents removed their children and found other alternatives. Chris and his brother were there for the duration of the school year.

Gregory in Summer School

At the end of the Eighth Grade, Gregory had not successfully completed one of his English classes. I decided to send him to summer school to pick up the English credit so that he could promote to high school. To do this, I canceled him out of the summer school program that I signed him up for at Texas Southern University (TSU). The program at Texas Southern University provided for a half day of instruction in reading and math five days a week. For the afternoon, Gregory would participate in various sporting and leisure activities.

Douglass Junior High conducted summer school that year. I paid for the classes and for the bus to take Gregory from his home school to Douglass. By this time, Gregory had started playing hooky from school and near the end of the class he was in danger of failing if he missed anymore class time. I found out how many absences and late arrivals he had left and started taking him to the school and dropping him off at the door. However, he did not pass. He claimed he went to class, but the teacher said he had not been there.

I went to Minter City Junior High school to find out what we needed to do to get Gregory signed up for the next school year. Then, the counselor informed me that at this time children did not have to be retained because they failed a class. I wish the counselor had given me that bit of information before, because had I known, I would have kept him in the other reading and math class that I signed him up for at Texas Southern University before I learned that he failed English. The TSU program may have been more beneficial since it focused on the basics; plus, I would not have lost money as I did when I withdrew Gregory from the TSU program.

Chris Needing a Change

The following year, Gregory entered high school but Chris continued at Minter City Junior High School. I started looking for a private school to send Chris to because he seemed headed for trouble, and I felt that he needed a different environment. On one occasion, the school expelled Chris for three days. When I asked one of the assistant principals about the circumstances leading to the expulsion, she expressed her suspicion that another child started a fight with Chris, but the other child would not admit to it, so the school expelled both boys. My concern centered around the long term implications of the expulsion. I had read an article in the newspaper, which indicated that a child's school file is permanently stamped across the front when the child is disciplined.

I took Chris to take the entrance test at Westbury Christian Academy. The administrator did not seem positive when I called to inquire about Chris' application for admission. Also, the school did not call me with the test results or an admissions decision. I feared that Chris was labeled as a behavioral problem and decided not to pursue that school further.

Chris followed in his brother's path at Minter City Junior High by studying music. He played the clarinet in Band. Mr. munson expressed that Chris had talent, but after the first year, Chris decided not to take band anymore. Instead, in the Seventh Grade, as he became eligible, he played basketball, football and participated in track and field events.

Unfortunately, during the time Chris was at Minter City Junior High School, his counselor discouraged him from taking college preparatory courses. When Chris completed his Eighth Grade class schedule, he selected Spanish and Algebra. The counselor changed his Spanish selection to Conversational Spanish and the Algebra to a general math class.

When I reviewed his schedule and saw the Conversational Spanish class, I asked Chris why he didn't just take Spanish. He explained that the counselor changed his schedule because she felt he should take Conversational Spanish first to see if he liked it. She, similarly, persuaded him that Algebra would be too tough for him. I felt despair and told Chris that I would call his counselor.

When I called the counselor regarding the conversation I had with Chris, she explained that she changed Chris' schedule to have Conversational Spanish because he had not taken any Spanish before, and she felt he would be at a disadvantage in the class. I asked the counselor how many years of Spanish the other children registered for the class had taken. She replied that the school offered Spanish to the students for the first time in Eight Grade. "Then he'll have the same advantage as everyone else.", I observed trying not to sound too sarcastic. I told the counselor that I wanted her to place the regular Spanish class back on Chris' schedule.

We also discussed the Algebra class, and I told her that I wanted Chris to take the Algebra instead of the general math class. The counselor called me back some days later to explain that Chris could not enroll in the Algebra class because it was canceled since too few students registered for it.

"You mean that with all the children at the school (the school was extremely overcrowded), not enough signed up for Algebra to be taught?", I asked incredulously.

She said not enough students showed interest. I, now, wonder if she deliberately prevented Chris from registering for the class or whether she simply discouraged enough of those students who wanted to register for the class to cause it to be canceled. I don't know.

Gregory in High School

The next year, Gregory attended Eagle High School. The teaching levels were basic, academic, and advanced. The school placed Gregory in basic level classes. At the first parent-teacher conferences, the teachers praised Gregory and applauded his performance, but shortly thereafter, his teachers related that his performance level dropped. This cycle of failure and limitation frustrated him and us. A few of his teachers said he needed to be consistent in doing his work in order to get out of the basic level classes. Although, he did not have a behavioral problem, some of his teachers said that in many of the basic level classes, they had behavioral problems that made effective teaching and learning difficult if not impossible.

As time passed, Gregory failed a few classes. In an effort to insure that he graduate from high school, I decided to send him to summer school to pick up part A and B of English 3. He needed to complete English 3 before he could be classified as a senior.

Summer school for the high schools was conducted at a central location. This particular year Colliers High School conducted the classes.

At the end of the English 3A class, Gregory did not bring home a grade report as scheduled. I wondered if he passed the class. When I questioned him, he said he didn't know if he passed; he said the instructor did not give him a report. I fussed at him for not having the report and for claiming the teacher did not give it to him.

My level of frustration about the situation rose and after getting to work, I called the school to find out if Gregory completed the class successfully. The person who answered insisted that the school gave a report to all of the students and that I should get the information from my child. I explained that he said he was not given a report, but whether he was given a report or not, I wanted to know if he passed or failed his summer school class.

Eventually, she transferred me a lady who identified herself as one of the principals of summer school. She got the file and said that Gregory told the truth. The report Gregory should have received was still in his file. She said he passed the class, and they would send that information to his home school. Breathing a sigh of relief, I asked if she was sure. She said she was sure because she had the report in front of her.

After I hung up from the school, I called Gregory and gave him the good news. I apologized for the fuss I made because he did not bring a report home. He thanked me for finding out that he passed the class. He said he was not sure how well he did on the final, but when the teacher did not give him a report, he began to worry that he had failed.

I did not leave work and go over to the school to pick up a copy of the report. I believed the information from the principal that he had passed the class and that the information would be sent to Eagle High School as she told me it would be. Gregory went on to take the second half of English 3 in summer school. He passed and brought home a report to that effect.

Regarding the first half of English 3, I later found out that the report sent to Eagle High School stated that he failed. However, a lot of time passed before I found this out. Nevertheless, I set out to get the record corrected. The school counselor told me I had to go to the administrative offices to get the grade corrected.

I went to the administrative offices and waited a few hours to discuss the situation with someone. The women I met with called around the district to locate the appropriate people who could help resolve this dilemma. She found one of the summer school principals who felt sure she remembered talking to me. However, she could not be certain of the grade on the report or what she told me at the time. For this reason and because Gregory's file now had a slip indicating that he failed, she told me that I needed to talk to Gregory's English 3A summer school class teacher.

The teacher, a burly man, worked at Kramer High School. I told him about the sequence of events leading to my finding out that Gregory passed the class. I repeated the conversation I had with one of the summer school principals who verified that Gregory passed the class. Obviously, I told him, a mistake was made because a report was sent to Eagle High School indicating that Gregory failed the class. The teacher took a defensive stance and said he remembered Gregory and that he certainly did not pass the class. He had no explanation for the principal finding a report in the file indicating that he passed.

I felt helpless. I did not drive over to the summer school office and pick up the report after talking to that principal. Gregory was not given a report. The school did not mail us a report. I had no proof and the teacher was not willing to correct the grade sent to Gregory's home school. I saw this as another case where a

White instructor saw the opportunity to victimize a Black child with impunity and did not pass up the chance.

The main area of consistency for Gregory during the first three years of high school was music. However, that area was plagued with problems as well.

Mr. Cornell, the band director, made sure the children understood that if they did not report early for Band during the summer, they would not be in the performing bands during the school year. No excuses were acceptable.

During the first summer, Gregory was supposed to report early for band practice, his paternal grandmother died. The funeral was held out of state, and I insisted that Gregory attend. Gregory explained that he would not be allowed in performing bands if he went to the funeral because those who did not report early did not get to participate. There were no excuses. I tried to get Gregory to realize that his teacher would understand that his need to attend his grandmother's funeral was not an excuse and that he should talk to Mr. Cornell. Gregory felt that he would be making excuses and didn't want to talk to Mr. Cornell. His fear prevented his discussion, and he could not play in the performing bands at the start of the school year. However, Mr. Cornell expressed that Gregory was performing extremely well in Band and moved him up to the performing bands later that year.

The second year Gregory did not have transportation to get to school during the middle of the day, so he did not report early. Again, Mr. Cornell placed Gregory in a holding class for those who, for whatever reason, do not make the performing bands. However, Mr. Cornell said that because Gregory performed well in music, he would move him up later in the year if he showed he could be relied upon to be available for practice and performances.

Later, when Gregory got the use of my car, Mr. Cornell moved him to one of the performing bands. Gregory achieved good reports during the first and second semester of the year. He kept up with his schedule and met his commitments. He made an A in band for the first semester of the school year and made an A in the first two grading periods of the second semester. I began to feel that maybe his music would move him out of the vicious cycle of failure which he experienced in many of his academic trials. Perhaps he was coming out of the woods.

Then, the Saturday after the last day of school, Gregory was supposed to perform with the Graduation Band. But, on the last day of school, his dad went to the school to get him. He was in a hurry to go out of town and wanted Gregory to go with him. He did not allow Gregory the time to go back into the school to inform his band director that he would miss the graduation commitment.

Later, when I requested a transcript of Gregory's grades, the official record showed that Gregory failed band for that entire year. I talked to the counselor about this. The report card that I had for the first semester showed that he made an A. For the second half of the year the report card showed that he made A's in the first two grading periods; however, I did not have a final report card showing the grade for the third and final grading periods. I asked the counselor why the official record was different from Gregory's report card. The counselor talked to the teacher and reported that he said a mistake was made on the first semester grade. Upon adjustment, he changed the first semester grade from F to B. For the second semester, he kept the grade as a F because he said Gregory did not take a final examination.

I asked Gregory why he did not take the final examination. He told me that if he met all of his commitments, he would not have to take a final exam. The fact that he could read and play the music at the performances was what he would be graded on. He said the teacher made it clear to the class before they got in the band that if they did not meet their commitments they would not pass the class. He did not meet the last commitment. He really felt ashamed about failing to show up for the graduation band performance. Although he had no control over the situation, Gregory felt that the teacher justifiably failed him for the entire semester because he missed one commitment; I stopped trying to get the second semester grade corrected. After that year, Gregory did not take Music.

A Change for Chris

During Chris' Eighth Grade year at Minter City Junior High school, his dad and the fathers of three other boys who played soccer with Chris discussed the possibility of enrolling their sons in Justin Regale College Preparatory School. The school had high academic standards and an excellent soccer program. I really felt that Chris needed a change in his school environment and readily agreed that it would be worthwhile for us to pursue this idea. None of the other boys went to junior high school with Chris, but two of the boys were in advanced level classes at the junior high schools they attended. Chris and the other three boys took the entrance exam during the second semester of their Eighth Grade year.

An article I read about Catholic schools indicated that a student needed to score better than 70 percent of the children taking the entrance exams city wide to maximize their chance of being admitted to their school of choice. Also, good grades and recommendations from members of the faculty at the student's previous school were important. Chris' grades were not the greatest and one of the teacher recommendations he received about his abilities was unenthusiastic and non-committal. However, the positive result Chris received on the entrance exam pleased us; he scored better than most of the children taking the exam city wide.

Fortunately, those making the admission decisions for Justin Regale College Preparatory admitted Chris since it was the only school he placed on his list of choices. (Those who made the admissions decision either judged the candidates fairly, were open minded, saw the need for a more diverse student body or for some other reason admitted Chris.) This was in spite of the fact that his prior academic performance was well below his potential as measured by standardized test and the fact that he had once been disciplined in middle school.

Low Expectations

The school also admitted the other three boys. One of the boys achieved an excellent score on the entrance exam and qualified for advanced level placement in his classes. This same boy also tested well enough on subject placement test to skip first year Spanish and Algebra. One of the other boys scored well enough for advanced level placement in some of his classes.

This change in school programs also marked a change for Chris in soccer. Chris had played club soccer since age 5. For the last several seasons, Chris played on a winning gold team. Chris and the three other boys were among the most skillful players on their team. The coach had made Chris captain of the team and gave him an arm band to denote it. However, when the team had tryouts for a gold cup team to represent the USA, none of the Black boys made it to the next level tryouts. I was surprised that none of the Black boys made it and a number of the White parents expressed that they were surprised too. After the tryouts were over, the coach took the arm band from Chris and gave it to one of the boys who made it to the next level of tryouts. I felt this was uncalled for because the tryouts were not directly related to team performance. Also the coach told Chris to come to the field several hours before game time. When I found that the coach wanted Chris to watch other games so he could show him good skills, I told Chris he would report to the field the same time as his fellow team members. I did not want the coach to undermine Chris' skill while trying to convince him that he did not pass the tryouts because his skills were inferior to those of his teammates. Chris had proven on the field that this was not the case. I was glad for Chris to leave the team because it was apparent that on that team, he would not be promoted to higher levels in soccer based on his ability.

9
Gregory at the Crossroads

Gregory's poor academic performance created a crisis for the family; he was not doing well in school at all. His dad suggested that we needed to do something to help Gregory or he just would not be able to make his own way in life. We had allowed him to linger in the system much too long without correcting his problems, and now we feared that it might be too late. Plus, Gregory had lost all confidence in his ability to get out of the academic rut in which he found himself.

I had already looked at a number of regular private schools and knew they would not permit Gregory to enroll because of his poor academic achievement and his failure to work at grade level. Others schools that may have taken him were either too expensive or were ruled out for other reasons. However, we heard about Memorial Hall High School and how they worked with children who were at various academic levels: above, below, and at grade level. We took Gregory there for evaluation. After the evaluation, we met with the school administrators. They did not overly encourage us, but they indicated a willingness to work with Gregory if we decided to enroll him. The program impressed us. However, we lived a long distance away from the school, and it was not practical for Gregory to get there on the bus. We would need another car, in addition to the tuition expense. These considerations caused us to put that option on a back burner, and Gregory continued to linger within the system.

A Name I Can't Read

Then one semester, Gregory successfully completed only one-half unit in school. I called the school's head counselor for advice and references for alternative school programs. She could not make a referral, but suggested that an important criteria for selecting a new school was the school's accreditation. After I looked at a few alternative schools without success, a friend told me about the school her son attended.

The school described its program as an alternative to the regular school concept. The school permitted the students a lot of flexibility. Within certain time limits, they could come to school as early or as late as they pleased as long as the daily time was contiguous. The school allowed the students to take several classes and offered the classes every hour, unless otherwise designated. The students could attend one class all day or attend multiple classes; however, the school counted all hours toward the total hours required for the month.

The school's concept and program sounded workable, and the school was on my way to work. I took Gregory to the school for testing and evaluation. After reviewing and discussing the results with the school, I enrolled Gregory in the program.

When I enrolled Gregory, he needed to complete about 5 units of regular curriculum classes to graduate from high school. He also needed to complete 2 additional units required to graduate from the new school.

At first, Gregory registered for algebra and history. He began his study by attending both classes; then he focused on the algebra all day and even studied diligently at home. He finished the algebra within a few weeks and then went back to focus in on the history class. He completed that class within a few weeks also. He completed a few more classes and continued to make progress until the summer. After the summer, Gregory took a job in the afternoon and his progress slowed. The school rules changed so that students were prevented from taking more than one class at a time. Gregory signed up for a class that had both lab and lecture. The lecture part of the class met in the mornings and the lab portion of the class met in the afternoon during Gregory's work hours. Gregory completed the lecture portion of the class and then stopped attending instead of adjusting his work hours. A lot of the flexibility had been taken out of the program, but since Gregory did not bring it to our attention, we were unable to address the problem. Meanwhile, Gregory got so far behind in his hours that it was not likely he could make them up. At that time, he still needed one and one-half units to graduate.

Gregory, now nineteen years old, still did not have the coveted "high school diploma". He found himself going to companies looking for work and finding that he could not apply for most jobs because he did not graduate from high school. He didn't know what to do, but he knew he wanted to be qualified to apply for some of the more desirable jobs. He landed a few jobs that paid more than minimum wage, but found that these jobs usually required a tremendous amount of physical labor for the wages, provided poor benefits, little job security, and little respect from management. Realizing that he needed a high school diploma, Gregory asked about going to night school at the local community college. However, he found that he would have to retake all of the classes that he completed at the alternative school because his poor attendance prevented him from getting credit for the classes he took there. He would have to begin his academic work where he was when he left Eagle High School.

Gregory decided to take the GED examination. We went to Houston Community College for him to sign up for GED classes, but we found the procedure for sign up was strange and confusing. Several years earlier, my nephew enrolled in the GED program and it appeared to be very straight forward at that time. Gregory decided to study for the exam on his own. When he got ready to sign up for the exam, we found that the procedure for that was also strange and confusing. When we checked on exam dates, no one seemed to have answers. Later, when we called back to get more information, we were told that if he wanted to take the next exam, he would have to rush down to pay by 5:30 that same day. I questioned why we were not given that information a few days before and allowed to pay at that time. It was like running an obstacle course instead of having a set definable procedure for those trying to get a GED. It made me wonder: what's going on with the GED program?

In January, after his twentieth birthday, Gregory sat for the GED examination and passed. He jumped for joy. But in his joy, Gregory realized that his reasonable expectation for work remained limited. He determined that it would be extremely difficult to get a good job without specialized skill training or a college education. Gregory expressed his desire to attend college. He, eventually, enrolled at Southern University in Baton Rouge to try to get the education needed to become better equipped in his struggle to realize the American dream. Gregory dropped out of Southern after about a year and took a truck driver course before returning to Houston to drive a truck for Astro Concrete.

10
Gregory, Nowhere to Hide

This chapter is written to point out how deeply ingrained racism is in our society and how it appears in our everyday interaction with one another. This book presents a look at how children are affected by biased attitudes in the classroom. But, the classroom is a microcosm of a larger society and self-esteem is often attacked as children participate in everyday activities that are not necessarily within the school system. The following are some activities that Gregory participated in and experienced disillusionment.

Swimming

Gregory started taking Red Cross swimming lessons after his third birthday. His swimming skills developed exceptionally well and he seemed to be a natural in the water. He took his first classes at the YMCA in Des Plains. When we moved to the east side of Elgin, he took classes at the YMCA and the YWCA. Gregory progressed well through the various Red Cross classes.

Gregory's last swimming class at the East side YMCA in Elgin was an advanced class. The instructor graded the children on the last day of class and gave us a skills report. Gregory's report showed that he mastered all of the skills listed; however, the instructor checked that he did not pass him to the next level. I thought this was a mistake and wanted to get the report corrected. Since Gregory's instructor was not available, I talked to his superior, who oversaw the testing and was still in the pool area. He did not know why the teacher did not promote Gregory. He agreed with the report that Gregory had mastered all of the skills listed for passing to the next level. He suggested that I wait for the instructor to come out of the locker room because he was sure he had not left the building.

When the instructor came out of the locker room, I went to him and calmly asked why he failed to promote Gregory to the next level even though he mastered all of the required skills. He replied that it wouldn't hurt Gregory to practice more. I pointed out that the children in the level below Gregory, which included Gregory's younger brother, were just promoted to the class that Gregory had just completed and these children's skill and performance levels did not nearly measure up to Gregory's. I did not want Gregory retained at a level where he demonstrated mastery of the skills required to pass to the next level.

As I pressed this point with the instructor, he explained that the next level required more work on the butterfly stroke. He said he, himself, was not strong enough with the butterfly stroke to teach Gregory how to further improve on his butterfly stroke. For this reason, he said there would be no use promoting Gregory to the next level, especially since the next level was not offered at the YMCA on our side of town.

I asked the instructor whether the West side YMCA offered the class for the next skill level.

He said, "Yes, and if Gregory can get to the West side YMCA, I'll promote him."

I was puzzled about why he felt that getting Gregory to the other YMCA was a problem; however, I promptly informed him that getting Gregory to the other YMCA did not pose a problem. He promoted Gregory and I registered him for the next level swimming class at the YMCA on the West side of town.

When we got to the West side YMCA for the class, I noticed that there were a lot of children there. (There had been only one other child in the class that Gregory had just graduated from on the East side.) Almost all of the children in the class at this YMCA were white. The atmosphere of this class was more like that of a swim team rather than a swimming class like the others Gregory had taken. The coaches assigned the children lanes and timed them. I thought about it and began to feel that a class conducted in this manner would be good for Gregory.

Unfortunately, Gregory's enthusiasm was short lived. He completed the class sessions, but when it was time for him to sign up for the next class, he begged me not to make him. I was confused about why he did not want to since he always enjoyed swim classes. However, I was not aware of any problems he may have had in the class because I spent his swim class time outside jogging on the dirt track instead of watching the lessons from the sidelines as I had done most of the time at the East side YMCA.

During our last summer in Elgin, I registered the children in Camp Wa-taw-ga-me. A private school on the East side of Elgin conducted this camp. This was the school I tried to enroll Gregory in when he had problems at Wren Lake Elementary School.

The school had an olympic size pool. It happened that one morning, I returned to the camp to tell Gregory something. A staff member directed me to the pool. Gregory was the only one in the pool. I observed a man standing on the sidelines timing Gregory as he did laps in the pool. I watched and waited until Gregory finished his laps. The man told me that Gregory had exceptional swimming ability and that in order to improve his endurance he had him swim a mile each morning.

When we moved to Minter City, a suburb of Houston, I wanted Gregory to become a part of an organized swim program. I took him to tryout for a swim team in Sugarland, Texas. The coach told Gregory to get in the water so he could see what he could do. I left him and went inside to inquire about the program details. When Gregory finished outside, I asked him what he thought about joining the swim team. Gregory drew up his shoulders while diverting his eyes from me.

Then he looked at me and said, "Mom, I don't see any Black people here."

I told him that he didn't see any right now, but if we came at another time he might see some. I looked around and found a group picture on one of the walls that had a Black person included in it. I showed it to Gregory. He looked at me as if to say, "You don't understand".

He said, "No, mom."

Reluctantly, I let the swim team issue drop. After that Gregory did recreational swimming but did not enroll in any formal swim classes, except for those conducted at the various day care camps he attended.

When Gregory became old enough to work as a lifeguard, he took the lifeguard training course at a YMCA in Houston. He successfully completed the class and worked as a lifeguard and swimming pool manager for a period of time.

Soccer

Gregory first started playing soccer with a soccer club in Elgin. When we moved to Minter City, we signed Gregory up with the Minter City Soccer Club. The program divided the teams based on the child's age. Gregory became a part of an already established team that had just enough boys as the number of players needed to play the game.

The coach motivated the team and the boys were determined and competitive. They took first place in the state competition that season. The newest team members, two black boys, Gregory and Danny, took turns making up the bench since the team usually had only one extra player. The coach pulled Gregory or Danny in and out of the game whenever the other one made a mistake or failed to get the ball. This made their failures the prominent focus or justification for the coach's decision to bench them. The other players usually played the whole game regardless of their failures or mistakes in judgement.

At the end of the season, the club held its awards ceremony. The various coaches introduced their players, made comments about each child, and presented the team and individual awards. Eventually, Gregory's coach introduced his players. He made the statement that he had seen and heard various philosophies on how to introduce players. However, he said that he was going to introduce his players by the positions they played. He called out the position and then called out the player who played the position. He called Gregory last. Gregory played right wing. I thought, "If right wing does not come before any other position, it should come before left wing." I was painfully reminded of the "name I can't read" incident where Gregory received all of his papers last.

When the coach talked about performance, he singled Gregory out and asked if he made even one goal the entire season. Luckily, Gregory was able to say, confidently, "yes, don't you remember.....".

Later, when the coach needed players for a new team, he called to see if Gregory would join the team. I told Gregory the coach wanted to talk to him about joining his new team. Gregory asked me to tell the coach he didn't want to play. Instead, I told the coach he could talk to Gregory himself. Gregory's answer remained "no."

II
Avoiding the Pitfalls

Chris entered Justin Regale for Ninth Grade and had a real challenge ahead of him. Hard work and serious study were among the ingredients necessary for him to succeed. Chris needed to work at breaking the cycle of underachieving in his studies.

Chris was focused and tenacious as he developed his skill and abilities in football, soccer and track. Chris and the three boys who enrolled at Justin Regale with him all played varsity soccer while there. As a part of the team, they were a dynamic force and they all lettered in that sport.

Chris maintained average grades while at Justin Regale. However, he regained a good measure of his self-confidence and a renewed belief in his ability to do well academically. He began to exhibit his aptitude for math and science, as he did well in algebra, chemistry, physics and advanced math concepts. His potential in oral and written communications began to shine through, as well. Mrs. Yantzen, his English 2 and English 4 teacher, recognized his speaking and writing ability and provided him with a tremendous amount of encouragement. I am sure this encouragement boosted his confidence and proficiency level.

In spite of everything that was positive for Chris at Justin Regale, he encountered a situation that he could not effectively handle and should have talked about with us or school administrators. The situation occurred during Chris' second year at Justin Regale when he was enrolled in a science class. At the first progress reporting period Chris was doing well in the class; then, he began to do poorly. He asked to go to the homes of other students to get notes from this science class. This upset me because I felt he should have his own notes. He complained that his eyes bothered him, but the eye doctor reported no change in his eye condition. Chris needed to continue making adjustments as previously instructed by his doctor.

At each successive progress reporting period, Chris' progress report in the science class was not good. I talked with his teacher in an effort to get to the root of the problem. Finally, I found that Chris scored well on his homework and tests based on the textbook, but he failed the test that were based on the board work. I learned that the board work problem developed when the teacher changed where Chris sat in the classroom. At the beginning of the school year, there was open seating and Chris chose a seat at the front of the classroom with a clear view of the blackboard. Then the teacher moved him to a position in the back of the room where he did not have a clear view of the board work. Chris said that he told the teacher about his eye problem and his need for an unobstructed view of the blackboard. However, he said the teacher did not want to discuss it and told him to sit down in his new seat. The teacher frequently put critical information on the board and subsequently tested on it. Chris failed the tests based on the board work and his overall grade suffered. By the time I finally pinpointed the cause for his low grade, the school year had nearly ended.

I went back to school and explained the details of what I had learned to the teacher. The teacher said he did not realize Chris had a vision problem because the problem was not apparent when he played sports. He said that because Chris did so well in the class at the beginning of the school year and another student did poorly, he moved the other student to Chris' seat. When Chris talked to him about the seating, he said he did not believe him and dismissed his request as an attempt to sit where he wanted to sit. He sent him back to his new seat.

I explained to the teacher that Chris' eye problem was a matter of school record and that Chris took responsibility for making sure he got a seat that gave him a clear view of the blackboard and other written materials. Because he shouldered this responsibility, I did not become involved in the seat selection process. Therefore, it did not dawn on me that his classroom problems occurred because he did not have a seat with a clear view of the board work.

After our meeting, the teacher assigned Chris to a different seat. The new seat assignment provided a clear view of the blackboard, and he managed to pass the class.

This situation had an adverse affect on Chris' attitude about his ability to control his destiny. His increased stress and agitation levels were apparent during that period. His plans for traveling to Europe with the soccer team nearly collapsed because he almost failed the science class. Had he failed the class, he would have had to take the class again in summer school instead of going to Europe with the soccer team.

Sometime later, Chris and I talked about this incident and his difficulty in handling it. I wanted him to understand that when he encountered teachers who would not respond to his needs, he needed to seek assistance from us or school administrators to resolve the problem.

I felt personally saddened that Chris did not feel he could talk directly to me about his problems. Instead he dropped hints about needing to borrow the notes of other student and having problems with his eyes. When I did not agree for him to go to the homes of others for notes and had his eyes checked, he became silent and gave up seeking my help to resolve his problems in school. Signs of despondency creep into his demeanor.

However, deep down, I understood why he did not come to me. I had failed him in past situations. In kindergarten when he appealed for my help to get into a reading group, my efforts failed to get him the reading instruction he so badly wanted and needed. In first grade, all of my efforts to get him moved into a reading level were not realized until March, seven months after the school year began. When I noticed or was made aware of other problem situations, adjustments were made, but the problems were usually not resolved effectively. For instance, during his Fifth Grade year, my efforts caused the school to move him into the Advanced Math and Science class, but he was not placed in the Language Arts classes which supported the Advanced Math and Science classes. He missed instruction critical for completing his class work. In junior high, I continued to send him to the school during a period of extreme unrest.

The next situation is one that I struggle to write about. Whether the situation is based on bias, cruelty, or just the hard facts of life, those who have control over who will pass or fail can impact students negatively if that control is used unfairly. I decided to write about this incident so that those entering the teaching profession will realize that using deceptive tactics to fail students of a certain group can destroy children and do an injustice to society as a whole. Some students are placed in the embarrassing position of not being able to play sports because a teacher has strategically set a trap to fail them. Some students being fearful of the potential trap may decide not to play sports even before the games begin in an effort to save themselves the embarrassment of not being eligible to play due to failing grades. I hope reading about the following incident will cause teachers to avoid participating in practices that are designed expressly to fail students.

Early, during Chris' Eleventh Grade year, I went to the school for conference night. I did not receive a progress report for this particular class. However, I waited in line for a conference with the teacher for the class. I asked about Chris' progress and the teacher checked his record book which was already laid open on the table. During the first week of school, Chris made two failing grades represented by very low numerical scores. He scored a 10 on one of the test. After that week he received grades of 90 and above; the teacher said that he made the highest grades in the class. However, because of their weight, the two failing marks that Chris received during the first week of school caused his overall grade to be F. I asked the teacher if he planned to give any additional exams of sufficient weight to balance the two failing grades Chris received during the first week of school. He said he did not plan to. I sighed and observed that Chris had failed the entire grading period during the first week of school before he (the teacher) had a chance to really start teaching. Suspecting that the tests of the first week were a trap that this teacher has laid for Chris, I told him that there did not appear to be any redemption built into the system when a child could fail during the first week of school regardless of making A's at every opportunity given during the rest of the grading period. I told him that it had to be very stressful for a child to know that no matter how hard he studied or how well he performed on subsequent test and assignments given after the first week of school, he could not avoid failing during that grading period. I made these and a few other remarks to the teacher casually and calmly in light of my knowledge that the school was in mourning for a student who had committed suicide because of extreme stress believed to be brought on because of his grades. The teacher suggested that since a large number of the students failed the tests of the first week, he might give them the opportunity to do certain activities to have at least one low grade dropped.

When I returned home, I talked with Chris about his low test scores in that class during the first week of school and how those scores would affect his report card grade. He said that he knew those two low grades would keep his average at failing, but since there was nothing he could do about it now, he was trying his best to keep his grades up while waiting for the teacher to give him a chance to do extra work in order to have a low score dropped. I did not mention any of the observations or suggestions that I made to the teacher to Chris because I felt that those comments would not be productive or helpful to him. Instead, I encouraged Chris to continue to do his best in the class so that if the teacher gave him the opportunity to do extra work for a grade to be dropped his other grades would be high enough to raise his average to a passing grade.

I suspected the teacher would ignore the failing grades of the first week for those students he did not wish to fail. I was surprised at this young teachers actions because he had always spoken so highly of Chris. This teacher's ploy to deliberately fail Chris and make him feel that he was justified in doing so was particularly cruel. I can but imagine the helplessness and over-whelming stress that Chris felt as the possibility of receiving a failing grade loomed over his head.

There is tremendous pressure to pull a child off the playing field and prevent him from playing sports as soon as the possibility of a failing grade becomes apparent. Parents at sporting events often asked about Chris' grades and expressed their opinion that if a child's grades are not exemplary, he should be required to stay off the field until the grades improved. Yet, I felt that as long as Chris remained eligible to play, I would not prevent him. I felt that he needed sports as an outlet as he coped with the bias and preju-dice that he encountered even at his tender age.

Year after year, I saw evidence of the trap set before Chris. I saw it as I talked to one of his teachers during his freshman year. The teacher said, "Chris works hard. He comes and talks to me about how he can improve his grade, but he just can't seem to get it."

I listened to the vagueness of his comments and sensed the undeniable presence of the trap. I, also, perceived the icy walls of the trap as I had a conference with one of Chris teachers dur-ing his junior year. However, I did not feel that this teacher in-tended to outright fail Chris, but to make a statement that he could not rise above a given level no matter what he did, and there was no need to discuss it. (From the first conference, I felt that a C was the highest grade Chris could receive from this teacher regardless of how he performed.) I continued to conference with this teacher to show support for my child. I even commented to Chris that I knew what he must be going through in dealing with closed minds. Chris did not dwell on the subject, but acknowledged the fact. I think he realized that there were certain teachers who would not acknowledge or encourage his talents, and he relished those who did.

The point that I want to make is that to deliberately fail a child is not just cruel; it can destroy a child. I am sure we all will agree that too many children fail on their own and that those who try to excel should be encouraged and assisted at every opportunity. "A mind" is indeed "a terrible thing to waste."

In spite of the problems, I believe Chris was enriched by his years at Justin Regale, and I think he established a number of lasting associations and friendships there. Chris participated in many school activities. The student body elected him president of his senior class and the school administrators appointed him to serve on the school's discipline board. Chris graduated from Justin Regale in 1992 and went off to the University of Minnesota.

During Chris' senior year, while Jim Wacker was head coach at Texas Christian University, he recruited Chris to play football. After Coach Wacker accepted the head coaching position at the University of Minnesota, the recruiters talked to Chris about going there. He signed to go there on an athletic scholarship. Chris played varsity football that fall and for the next three years. In his studies, Chris, periodically, made the dean's list.

12
Contrasts and Comparisons

This book chronicles my two boys as they try to gain a meaningful education within several different school systems. In this chapter I point out the similarities and differences between what happened to my two sons and evaluate the result of what happened as it relates to their current educational and life situations. I present the elementary school grades separately and then look at the junior high and high school periods as a composite. Based on what happened to each child, I offer three factors that make the difference.

Kindergarten
Gregory - Live Oak Elementary, Mt. Prospect, Illinois - Gregory was removed from the classroom each morning during socialization time. Allegedly, he was removed because he did not know his letters, numbers and colors. However, I was aware that he knew those things before he was old enough to go to kindergarten. In talking to the special teacher that he went to when he was removed from the classroom, I concluded that no meaningful progress was made during the time he was removed. The special teacher said that he did nothing for her. However, when, at my suggestion, she asked him to write the letters of the alphabet and his numbers on a piece of paper for her, he did so. So far as what transpired in the class during the rest of the day, I do not know, but

judging from what I witnessed at the Christmas party, it was not positive. Instead, I'm sure it was extremely damaging to Gregory's positive feelings about himself. During the rest of his Kindergarten year, no problems were reported to me.

Chris - Wren Lake Elementary, Elgin, Illinois - Chris was excluded from reading groups during his Kindergarten year. Chris told me that his teacher was teaching his classmates to read, but that she was not teaching him. His teacher denied that she was teaching any of the children to read. During that year, Chris scored in the top 10 percentile of all children in the district taking the Metropolitan Readiness Test. The Summer after his Kindergarten year, I taught Chris to read. We started at the beginning of a reading program and his tutor continued it when he went to First Grade.

First Grade
Gregory - Live Oak Elementary, Mt. Prospect, Illinois - Gregory's teacher reported that he was in the second highest reading group.

Chris - Wren Lake Elementary, Elgin, Illinois - Chris was not taught to read in First Grade along with his classmates. He was placed in a pre-reading level and kept there for seven months of the school year. This is in-spite of the fact he was able to read when he started First Grade and the fact that he scored in the top 10 percentile of all children in the district taking the Metropolitan Readiness Test while in Kindergarten. We requested help from the district. The district reading coordinators tested Chris and he was successful through Level 7, which is 5 levels above where the school had placed him. In the meeting to discuss the district test results and placement, Chris was placed in Level 6. This was contrary to the publisher's guidelines which suggested that children should be placed a level above the level where they scored 80 percent or above. This compromise was made because of all the skill building instruction the school said he missed by being in Level 2. We also had Chris tested by an independent testing service and their testing indicated that his ability to perform academically exceeded his grade level in all areas. It also indicated his readiness for reading at Holt Level 8 and suggested that he should be in an advanced level math program. By this time the school was overtly hostile and we feared they were not willing to teach our children at any level. We sought to find another place for our children to attend school.

Second Grade
Gregory - Wren Lake Elementary, Elgin, Illinois - Gregory changed schools for Second Grade because we moved to another city. Shortly after school started, I discovered that Gregory was being removed from the classroom during reading time. The teacher gave the excuse that the other children were in reading groups together before and she did not want to put Gregory with them without special help. The women who took Gregory from the classroom were neighborhood mothers called "Super Moms". They were not given any work for Gregory and they did not give him any work to do. They isolated him in a room and watched the door while he was robbed of an education. Upon learning about this, I involved the Principal of the school and he promised to place Gregory in a reading group. Later, I learned that the reading group the Principal placed Gregory in was functionally non-existent. The reading group never met. It consisted of a girl who rarely came to school due to medical problems, and a Spanish boy who did not speak English. After that discovery, Gregory was supposedly placed in a reading group with his home room teacher. At the end of the school year, Gregory's teacher wanted us to agree for her to retain him, but I felt another year with her would be even more detrimental.

Chris - Brentwood Christian Academy, Des Plaines, Illinois -
At first they placed Chris at a reading level that was too low, but

they moved him up after I requested that they test and evaluate him for placement at a higher reading level. He did well and even made the honor roll on occasion.

Third Grade
Gregory - Wren Lake Elementary, Elgin, Illinois - In Third Grade Gregory completed Holt level 9 which is probably graded as a Second Grade book.

Chris - John Smith Elementary, Minter City, Texas - Chris' first teacher at John Smith Elementary failed to issue him a book and required that he wait for other students to complete their work and then borrow a book from one of the other students. She sent a note home requesting payment for the book she never issued and complained that he was not doing all of his work. When I went to discuss the book and the work that was not done, I found that he was placed at a Second Grade level for reading. This surprised me since the Principal told me they placed new students according to placement test, and Chris always tested above grade level. Upon requesting that they place Chris according to test scores, Chris was moved from that first teachers classroom altogether.

Fourth Grade
Gregory - Wren Lake Elementary, Elgin, Illinois - We hired a tutor who placed Gregory in Holt Level 10 for reading. The school placed Gregory, out of the schools reading material, at a reading level equivalent to Holt Level 4. Level 4 is five levels below where he successfully achieved in Third Grade and would be graded as a Kindergarten or First Grade textbook. Gregory was removed from the regular classroom for reading. After this discovery, the Principal told me that they gave Gregory a test which indicated he should be in Level 4, so they placed him in Level 4. I went to the district for help regarding the drop in Gregory's reading instruction level, but that was to no avail. After the middle of the

school year, we had Gregory and his brother tested by an independent testing service. The testing service test results indicated Gregory's readiness for Holt Level 11, which was consistent with where the tutor instructed him at the time.

Chris - John Smith Elementary, Minter City, Texas - Chris' teacher complained about him and his work in general terms and I was not able to put my finger on the problem. This teacher failed to give Chris class work assignments for the days he missed when he was sent home by the school nurse and she gave him zeroes for it. After telling her it was unfair for her to turn his A's into F's because of work she did not give him, she agreed to allow him to complete the work. Sensing that this teacher had a negative attitude toward Chris, I waited for the school year to end so he would be out of her class.

Fifth Grade
Gregory - Brentwood Christian Academy, Des Plaines, Illinois - and John Smith Elementary, Minter City, Texas - At the Academy, Gregory's teacher worked with him in the classroom along with the other students. We enrolled him in the after school tutoring program. Although his teacher had good things to say about Gregory's progress, his grades were terrible. At the end of the school year, Gregory's teacher told me that Gregory made great progress and she felt he would be able to perform in the Fifth Grade on his own the following year. She suggested that Gregory be retained in the Fifth Grade. She recommended that we place him in the Westbury Christian Academy since we planned to move to the Houston area. However, we could not get Gregory into Westbury Christian Academy because, as one of the administrators advised, applicants had to be at grade level and successful academically in their previous school. We enrolled Gregory in the local public school where he repeated the Fifth Grade. The school tested him and said he would be taught in Fifth Grade classes. Gregory's math teacher did not issue him a book and

161

withheld a book from him during the time he was supposed to do class work from the book. He became desperate about getting a book to start his work and wrote his name in a book that the teacher let him use. She, then, humiliated him by loudly accusing him of stealing a book in front of all the fifth grade classes in the open area. She later apologized to him, in private, after it was determined that she never issued him a book.

Chris - John Smith Elementary, Minter City, Texas - House Bill 72 went into effect just as Chris was about to enter Fifth Grade. House Bill 72 mandated that children be placed, for the language arts and the math and sciences, according to test scores achieved on the IOWA Test of Basic Skills or by teacher recommendation. Chris scored at the academic level for language arts and at the advanced level for math and sciences. However, the school placed Chris at the academic levels for all of his classes. After several attempts to find out how his placement related to his test scores, the counselor informed me that he was placed based on teacher recommendation. The teacher who made the recommendation was his fourth grade teacher. The one that I felt had a negative attitude toward him. Since no reasons were given for the recommendation, I requested that they place Chris according to his test scores. As a result, when he was moved up in the math and sciences, he was moved up in the language arts, as well. The counselor said that he was initially placed at a level below where he scored for the language arts. Chris had problems after the move because the school did not place him in the english class that went along with his science class and some to the work from the english class accounted for part of the science grade. Since I was not aware of the mix-up, this caused a division between Chris and me. I put pressure on Chris when his science teacher complained about him not doing the work from the english class. The school year was almost over before I inadvertently learned the cause of the problem from Chris' language arts teacher.

Contrasts and Comparisons

Junior High School

Gregory - Minter City Junior High, Minter City, Texas - Gregory struggled to get through Junior High School. However, his Music and Art teachers identified his ability in the areas of Music and Art. During his years in junior high, Gregory was slated to be taught at the "basic" level.

Chris - Minter City Junior High School, Minter City, Texas - Chris' counselor took Spanish and Algebra off his schedule for Eight Grade. After I talked to her about the classes, she put the Spanish back on his schedule. However, she claimed he could not take the Algebra class because the school did not have enough students interested for the class to be taught. Spanish and Algebra are classes that students should be strongly encouraged to take when it is expected that they will go on to college. Apparently, the counselor did not expect Chris to attend college, but, he must have scored high enough on standardized test so she could not be forthright and say he could not be scheduled for those classes. Instead she under-handily removed the classes from his schedule. Chris took band and started to participate in track, basketball and football while in Junior High. When Chris went to Junior High the school environment was very oppressive due to an administration that did not identify with the children. The administrators were still mostly white, and the student body was now predominantly black as Blacks moved in and Whites moved out of the area. During his Eighth Grade year, Chris took the Entrance Examination to get into a private school. It was apparent that he was at a critical point and in desperate need of an environment change to help him break out of a system that was slowly but surely stifling him academically, emotionally and spiritually. I did not have a problem with Eagle High School per se, but it was within the system and the way you go in is more likely the way you'll come out. Low aspirations due to low expectations.

163

High School
Gregory - Eagle High School, Minter City, Texas - and The Alternative Academy, Houston, Texas - In high school Gregory continued to be taught at the basic level. Finally, when it became apparent that Gregory probably would not complete high school at his regular school, we placed him in an alternative school. Initially, he showed promise by successfully completing a number of classes like Algebra, History, and Biology with A's. However, with a change in school policy that we were not aware of, Gregory got too far behind in his hours to get credit for any of the classes he completed. The school's policy changed to allow students to take only one class at a time. The lab portion of Gregory's class conflicted with his work schedule and he stopped going to class instead of trying to resolve the schedule conflict with the school.

Chris - Justin Regale College Preparatory, Houston, Texas - Chris tested well enough to get into a College Preparatory school. In the college preparatory school, Chris experienced enough academic success to regain confidence in his ability to do well academically. He served as president of his senior class and was appointed to the school's discipline board. He participated in several sports including soccer, football and track. Chris graduated from high school in 1992.

The Boys Today
Gregory - At his twentieth birthday, Gregory sat for and passed the exam to get a GED. After working a couple years, Gregory enrolled in college at Southern University in Louisiana. He attended for over a year and then dropped out. Before returning to Houston, he successfully completed a truck driving course. Upon returning to Houston, he took a job as a truck driver for Astro Concrete. Gregory now owns a trucking company and works toward making it a successful business venture. I wish him the very best.

Contrasts and Comparisons

Chris - After graduation from high school, Chris went on to the University of Minnesota. He received a football scholarship and played college football from 1992 through 1995. He, also, participated in indoor track. He received numerous honors in both sports. He was the 55 meter champion for the "Big Ten" colleges in the 1995-96 indoor track season. During his junior year he broke the school record for yards rushing in football. During his senior season, he was an official candidate for the Hiesman trophy. He acted as co-caption of the football team during his junior and senior seasons. In football, he received an award for the greatest contribution to the university at the end of his senior football season. In April of 1996, Chris was drafted into the NFL by the Green Bay Packer as a running back in the fourth round (way to go baby). Unfortunately, Chris incurred a shoulder injury during their first pre-season game. Yet, his team is the champion of Super Bowl XXXI!!!. How exciting. Chris is now married and takes classes during the off-season in an attempt to complete his undergraduate studies. I wish him the very, as well.

Contrasting the two Boys

In contrast, Gregory did not graduate from high school, but got a GED. (Getting a GED is an important step in going on with the rest of your life for educational and employment pursuits. It really does make a difference and opens up a world of opportunities for those who are in need of it.) Chris graduated from high school. Both boys went to college, however Gregory dropped out and Chris is close to getting an undergraduate degree.

Considering that both boys were excluded from the teaching/learning process during the primary grades, What makes the difference? In hindsight, I would say the difference lies in three areas.

First is awareness of what is happening. For Gregory, we allowed ourselves to believe that his exclusion from the classroom was an isolated occurrence rather than a pattern of intentional exclusion from the teaching/learning process. The signs of willful discriminatory exclusion were all there. The teacher smiled and gave a good report while she removed Gregory from the classroom. We did not want to believe his exclusion had nothing to do with what he knew or his ability to learn. We were not in tune with the fact that discriminatory, exclusion practices of this nature are commonplace against minority children and that it would likely happen again and again to Gregory and then to his brother. We failed to realize the fact that when we tried to help Gregory with the things he did not know or do in school, we were building only on what he knew and understood on his own, because he was not being taught in school. When the teacher said he was not doing well in school, I wanted to know what they were doing so that I could help him with that problem. Off course, his teacher could not give me papers on what he did since he was being excluded. We tried to fill in the holes, but we did not know where they all were. It was hit and miss because when a child is excluded from the teaching/learning process, he is missing most everything and he needs to be taught with that in mind.

With Chris being our second child, we had learned a little something from what happened to Gregory. Also, with Chris, we were aware of his superior performance on the Metropolitan Readiness test and this affirmed that he was ready to be taught. Therefore, when, in First Grade, we were told that he was not being taught because he was not ready, we knew better and tried to get help from the district.

The second factor is the timing of when support is provided for the child. For Chris, support was provided at an earlier stage. When the school did not teach Chris to read in Kindergarten, we taught him to read the following summer. We did not try to see what he did not know in order to know what to teach, we assumed he needed to be taught everything. By teaching everything from the reading program, Chris gained a firm foundation that he could build on and be confident about. He gained the skill needed to pass test given by the district to assess him. However, equally important is the fact that Chris had a tutor early in his situation and the tutor worked with him in the areas of Reading and Math during part of the time the school excluded him from the teaching/learning process. By having this early support, Chris' instruction/grade level as measured by standardized test was not allowed to drop as much as it would have without any instruction. The instruction he received helped him to maintain his performance level.

Gregory, on the other hand, was excluded from the classroom in Kindergarten and Second Grade and did not have a tutor to provide a program designed to give him the instruction needed for him to remain on target. He did not get a tutor until he reached the Fourth Grade. This meant that Gregory missed a lot of instruction and did not have an alternate means of getting the instruction needed to maintain a level of proficiency during that critical period. In talking to a Third Grade teacher recently, she told me about two students in her class who go to resource class for reading. She said that they read on a Second Grade level and that they are learning. When asked where they will be at the end of the year, she said that, as normal children, she expects them to be reading at Third Grade. She does not expect them to catch up with their classmates. Why not? She expressed that when children are either not taught or do not learn, their educational growth is stunted and they will likely remain behind their classmates unless direct measures are taken to correct their problems and bring them to grade level. She volunteered that the discrepancy in the reading level is also reflected in the class work that the students are required to do in the regular classroom. Many times when children are in low level classes, they cannot see their way out without help even when they have the ability. Even when test results show that they have the intelligence, if they do not perform no one will question their placement in lower level classes by teacher recommendation. The point is that children who get behind their classmates will have a problem not just with class work at grade level, but they may not catch up with their classmates. To catch up they will have to put forth extra effort and be taught with the intent of catching up.

Thirdly, early removal of the child from the environment or class that excludes him/her is critical. The child should be taken out of the class where he is not being taught and be placed where he will be taught. Otherwise, the situation compounds itself and becomes chronic. That is what happened to Gregory. He went off to kindergarten bright-eyed and ready to learn. Instead, he was removed from the classroom and/or denied a book to prevent him from learning. This pattern of discriminatory exclusion continued as Gregory went from class to class until he eventually could not help himself out of the abyss because of stunted educational growth due to a lack of instruction in the early grades and therefore a lack of confidence in his ability to excel. Also, because of academic deficiencies that developed over the years, it became easy for those against him to make him feel inferior academically. When children are not taught in Kindergarten, First and Second Grade, they will be looked upon as low achievers, because they will not be able to perform effectively. They will no longer have to be discriminated against in order to be excluded for the regular mainstream classroom. To regain their footing, they will have to receive the kind of help that will address what they really need. They need the basics skills which should have been taught and reinforced in the early school grades.

Chris was removed from the discriminatory exclusion situation much earlier than Gregory. Chris left the school that was excluding him at the end of First Grade. Whereas, Gregory remained in that system of exclusion until the end of the Fourth Grade. I must tell you that even with a tutor, you need to get the child out of school environments and classes that exclude them from the teaching/learning process. Children have to be taught in the classroom. That's where they are tested and graded and they need to succeed where they are so they will keep their self-confidence and maintain their self-esteem. There are so many angles that teaching can take and children need to be exposed to the method that will be used to test them. It's fine to say, "he's doing well at home", but the report card is based on what he does in the classroom. I cannot emphasize enough that the primary years are critical. If children are not taught in the primary grades, they will not be able to perform until they get the instruction needed to unlock the mystery of learning.

Just to lend some insight on how critical it is for a child to be successful in some of the things he does, I want to share the following story. When Gregory went to the alternative school, he took Algebra and did well in it. He was excited that, with the instructor there to explain things that he did not understand, he was able to master the subject matter. He did the same thing with a History and a Biology class. Gregory was proud of his accomplishments. One day, I heard as he and his brother talked. Gregory expressed how good it felt to make a few good grades. Chris said, "Isn't it funny. When you make good grades, you get use to it, you realize that you can do it and it feels good. Making good grades is contagious."

13
Current Day Case Studies

This is a wake up call for those of you who may be sleeping and feel that traumatic events like what happened to us do not happen anymore. I write with the hope that my experiences will make you aware that your children could easily find themselves excluded from the educational process through no fault of their own.

I have listened as other parents tell about events that have impacted their children within the last several years, and I want to share their comments to heighten your awareness.

Case Study I

One mother, who has a husband and two children, told me the following story. They live in Lake Olympia which is a suburban area in Southwest Houston. Her daughter learned to read before she attended Kindergarten. She read so well that her Kindergarten teacher allowed her to read to the other children during story time. This mother became concerned about whether the teacher academically challenged her daughter because the work she brought home from school did not reflect the high academic achievement attributed to the school. The mother felt that the papers her daughter brought home indicated instruction at a low level. This mother discussed the situation with her daughter's teachers, and during the conference, her concerns were confirmed. The teacher explained that the children who attended Kindergarten for the half-day that her daughter attended were the slower children. The teacher apologized for failing to explain this to her before. Since this mother was a housewife at the time, she simply changed the time of day that her daughter attended Kindergarten. This mother felt that using the time of day as a method of determining which children would be taught at a low level did not sound logical or responsible; however, she accepted this explanation for the school failing to teach her child. She trusted that her daughter would be taught at a more appropriate level in the class conducted at a different time of day.

Here a brilliant child with great potential could become educationally handicapped simply because the school was not teaching her at a level appropriate to her ability or comparable to her peers. These parents should vigilantly watch their daughter's educational progress to insure that the school does not rob her of her potential for academic, social, and economic excellence at an early age.

Case Study II

Another mother chatted with me about her daughter's successful completion of Kindergarten at a private day care. In the next academic year, this mother registered her daughter in a public school. The public school allowed children who completed Kindergarten at a private day care to enroll in First Grade, even if the child was not old enough to attend Kindergarten in public school the prior year. However, this mother decided to have her daughter repeat Kindergarten at the public school in case her level of emotional maturity was not sufficiently developed due to her younger age. Soon after her daughter began school, the teacher complained about the child's inability to do the work. However, the teacher did not clearly explain the problem or give the mother suggestions to assist in correcting the problem. This mother felt that the teacher nitpicked and became frustrated. She waited for the school year to end. To add to the confusion, her daughter's eyeglasses mysteriously disappeared from the classroom. A substitute teacher later discovered the child's glasses in the teacher's desk. This mother wondered if the disappearance of the eyeglasses was more than just a coincidence.

Case Study III

One of the women who read my manuscript told me this story about her niece. Her brother and his family moved to a different area of the city and changed the school that his daughter attended. At her previous school, the daughter was enrolled in advanced level classes because of her performance on standardized test. However, the new school recommended that the brother allow them to place his daughter in academic level classes to counter any stress that might be caused by changing schools. The school suggested that when the child tested again, they would place her accordingly during the next school year. She told me that because she read my manuscript, she reasoned that her niece would probably lose proficiency by being placed in the lower level classes and advised her brother to insist that his daughter continue in advanced level classes according to her current test scores. This is an example of a child who could have lost testing proficiency due to a lack of exposure to advanced level concepts.

Case Study IV

In September 1995, my sister called me. She was very distraught. Less than a month before, she and her husband sold their home in Kansas City, Missouri, and moved to Monroe, Louisiana. They bought a house in a community which happened to be predominantly white. They registered their seven year old daughter in the Second Grade at the local elementary school. Shortly thereafter, the school informed them that they wanted to put their daughter back into the First Grade because she was not yet reading. My sister explained she was aware her daughter was not reading, and that in the Kansas city school, where their daughter attended, they taught Language Arts and did not formally start teaching reading until Second Grade. She further explained that her daughter was on the A/B honor roll in the school in Kansas City. Despite that fact, the new school was adamant that the child needed to be put back into the First Grade. My sister and her husband did not want their daughter put back because they felt she could catch up within a month or two if she received extra help. For that reason, my sister enrolled their daughter in a reading program with Sylvan Learning Center and hired a tutor. She requested that the new school allow the tutor to use material from the school's reading program. The school refused to allow the tutor the use of the schools reading resources stating that they could do nothing for the child unless they were allowed to put her back into the First Grade.

The teacher told my sister that even if her daughter could catch up it would not matter. The teacher explained that they would average the grades for reading from the first half of the school year, which they expected the child to fail, with the grades from the second half of the school year. They expected that the child would obtain an average grade of "D" or less. The teacher further explained that If a child obtained a "D" or less, the school required that the child repeat the grade. After observing in the classroom for three weeks, my sister felt convinced that her daughter would not be given any encouragement or assistance with reading in the Second Grade at her new school. Therefore, my sister and her husband closed up their house in Monroe and temporarily moved back to Kansas city to let their daughter attend Second Grade. They enrolled her in a supplemental reading program to further assure she would catch up in reading.

I talked to my sister approximately three weeks after their return to Kansas city and she told me that the Kansas City school her daughter attended still had not started teaching her to read. However, she told me that her daughter's most recent test scores from the supplemental reading program indicated that she had improved in reading from grade 1.3 to grade 1.9. They attributed this improvement to the supplemental reading program and the reinforcement work done at home.

Current Day Case Studies

I talked to my sister again at the beginning of the Christmas holidays and she told me that the school still had not started teaching their daughter to read. Her daughter's latest test scores from the supplemental reading program indicated her ability to read above grade 3. My sister indicated that the school continued to teach language arts to the children, instead of formally teaching reading. They told her that the children will usually become readers.

My sister said she found this approach hard to believe and sat in on several different classes because she felt she must be misunderstanding something. She observed in several classes and found that the teachers she observed read passages from the readers and then asked the associated multiple choice questions of the children. As the teachers calls out the multiple choice answers, they point to the answer choice. The children fill in the blank on the work sheet with their choice. From my sisters findings, this method is used until the end of Third Grade. In the Fourth Grade the children are on their own and some of them fail the grade largely because they cannot read. My sister found that there are a lot of fourth, fifth and sixth graders enrolled in the supplemental reading program with her daughter. She said that many of the parents are frustrated and angry because they thought the school was going to teach their children to read.

My sister and her family returned to Monroe after their daughter completed the Second Grade and the supplemental reading program. They again enrolled their daughter in the neighborhood school in Monroe. They are happy that their daughter is now on the Principal's list with a grade point average of 98.82. My sister thinks moving to Monroe is a blessing no longer in disguise. At least the problems associated with their daughter not being taught to read were discovered before she failed or developed bad habits to compensate for the inability to read.

I cringe when I think about those parents who cannot pay for supplemental reading programs as their children linger in Fourth Grade or Special Education programs until they dropout of school or get passed on without knowing how to read. Also, think how these children must suffer in other academic areas because they are unable to read at the instructional level of their other classes. My sister's findings are incredible and shed volumes of light on the question of why there are so many children who can not read.

My sister and her husband's response to the situation is an example of the extreme measures that parents will take to correct academic problems and to prevent their children from having academic problems. When academic problems are left unresolved, social problems will be in the backlash. My sister's findings point out that the cause and effect of illiteracy are bigger than the parent of the children directly damaged.

Case Study V

This example cuts to the very core of the larger problem. A co-worker, who read my manuscript, came to talk to me about a situation that seemed like deja vu in light of the incidents she read about in my manuscript. Her sister who lives in Katy, Texas enrolled her two year old daughter in a private day care. The daughter was the only Black child in her group. Her sister told her that one day, when she went to pick her daughter up from day care, she looked in through the window and noticed that all of the children were on a large pillow watching a movie. The teacher took the daughter off the large pillow and put her on a small pillow by herself. On another occasion, her sister went to the day care early and went to get her daughter from dance class. She paid an additional fee to enroll her daughter in the dance class, but found her not in attendance. The other members of the class were doing their dance steps. She asked why her daughter was not there and the teacher told her that her daughter was not in a good mood. The teacher went out to the playground and brought the daughter in. The daughter fell right in step with the other children. No signs of a bad mood. On another occasion, at a school Christmas party, the children brought gifts to exchange. The gifts were numbered and the children pulled numbers to determine which gift they were to receive. The gift the daughter brought was given the number 7. A boy in the class pulled the number 7, but the teacher did not give him the gift with the number 7 on it. When all the children had received gifts, the gift with the number 7 was left. The mother asked the teacher why she did not give the gift her daughter brought to the boy who pulled the number 7. She did not receive a response that she felt was satisfactory and expressed that it is time to look for other child care alternatives. This situation shows how ingrained and damaging racism is in our society. It starts to eat away at our children's sense of self-worth and esteem before they can understand the dynamics of what is happening to them.

Case Study VI

Another mother told me this story about her son. She enrolled her son in a private day care and kept him there through First Grade. He was an honor student. She planned to enroll him in another private school for the next school year and wondered what grade he should go into because he would not become 7 years old until December. The teacher at his school suggested that he was ready and should be placed in Second Grade. The teacher noted that the new school used the Spalding Reading Program and they did not. So, over the Summer, the mother hired a tutor to introduce the Spalding Reading program to her son. The following school year, she enrolled her son in the other private school which happened to be predominantly white. The administrator expressed that she wanted the son to repeat First Grade, but policy did not require it and the mother enrolled him in Second Grade. The son made all A's and B's. However, when they returned from the Christmas holidays, a new teacher took over his class. The administrator asked the mother to come to the office along with the new teacher. The administrator explained that her son would not pass to the Third Grade and gave no explanation beyond that. Since this was explained in front of the new teacher, the mother felt that the new teacher would have to fail her son. She told them that she was going to remove her son from the school. The administrator told her that she would be breaking the contract if she removed him, but the mother contended that the contract was broken by the school when they decided to fail her son even though he made good grades.

The mother enrolled her son in a public school. One day when she entered the building, she was stopped by one of the reading resource teachers. The teacher told her that her son was not responding in the reading resource class. The mother was surprised because no one advised her that her son was in reading resource class. She made an appointment with her son's teacher. She suspected the administrator from the private school talked to the officials of the public school and decided to take her son's report card to the meeting. She explained to the teacher that she removed her son from his previous school because the administrator there informed her that her son would not pass even though he made good grades. The teacher expressed that she was under the impression that she took him out of the private school because of learning difficulties. She showed the teacher her son's report card from the private school. After that her son was placed back in the regular classroom for reading, he responded and continues to make good grades.

The mother believes her son resented being pulled out of the regular classroom and expressed it by not responding in resource class. She was disturbed by his being placed in resource class without her knowledge. She fears that, since he was not responding, he could have been given a bad report and kept out of the regular classroom for years. This case shows how helpless children are when they are unfairly removed from the classroom and their parents are not made aware of it. The child can be labeled and setup for instruction at a level below his/her potential until he or she becomes a chronic underachiever.

Case Study VII

There are situations where parents do not have active involvement in their child's early educational development because they are not in the household with them. One man, who works as an electrical engineer and has two boys, told me about his situation. He was separated from his children and was not greatly involved in the schooling of his older child while he was in Kindergarten and First Grade and intermittently until he finished Sixth Grade. During that time, it became evident that his older child was going through an academic crisis and he made a commitment to do all he could to correct the situation. He expressed that he had a tough time dealing with the fact that his son was not successful in school because he, himself, had always excelled in school and learning came so easy for him. He related that it was hard for him not to take his son's problems in school as a personal failure and thus be patient with him as they worked to overcome his academic difficulties. He talked with his son's teachers at somewhat regular intervals since his older son was in some resource classes due to a learning disability and had been since the Second Grade. Some of the skills his son did not possess were so basic that he had to resist blaming the child and realize that he was not adequately exposed to those concepts while in resource classes. As he became increasingly involved with trying to correct his son's academic problems, he noticed that the teacher's expectations of his son increased. At the end of Seventh Grade, his son's teacher informed him that, based on test results and the ARD (Admission Review Dismissal) committee meeting, they wanted to place his son in all mainstream classes instead of keeping him in resource classes. They, also, placed his son in Algebra. The father said he could not understand the wisdom of that since he did not see evidence that his son had been taught the necessary concepts. However, true to his commitment, this father made himself available everyday to assist his son as he took on the higher level classes. He found the task to be overwhelmingly demanding

179

because of the math and language facts that his son was not adequately exposed to while in resource classes.

This father also expressed that he sometimes became frustrated while trying to assist his son with homework because he invariably found that he did not have all the necessary information available to him. For example, he related that he helped his son with an english assignment which required that he use a given set of words to write examples of a pun. For the word "wide", his son wrote, "At 350 pounds, he really was a Wide Receiver." The teacher marked that answer as incorrect along with another example of a pun. Each of the answers were worth 8 points and consequently, his son received 72 on the homework. As a result, this father wrote a letter to the teacher explaining that he helped his son to understand the concept of a pun and that he did not understand why the answers were marked as incorrect. The teacher called him and explained that she gave the children some other verbal instructions that were not printed on the work sheet. He explained to her how difficult it is for him to effectively help with homework when he tells his son to follow the instructions on the work sheet and there are verbal instruction that he is not aware of. The teacher called a second time to say she would grade the examples for a pun as correct and the grade was increased from 72 to 88.

In an effort to make studying a habit, this father set up a rigorous routine of study for his son, while trying to understand that it is a slow process that needs to allow his son time to enjoy some things other than study, study and study. He, also, had to realize that this was a big change for his son. He is now expected to learn and do a lot of academic work that was not required of him before. This father is certain that his efforts and the heightened expectations from the school will reap benefit for him and his son as well.

This case shows that there is hope even when the situation seems hopeless, if we make it a high priority to assure that the older child who has ended up in an academic rut makes it through. This will depend on the child letting go of his fear that he cannot learn and working diligently to take advantage of the help that is given. You can be assured that the child will need help getting to the point where he has confidence in his ability to learn, especially since he has been in an academic slump for an extended period. He will have to experience success many times before he begins to expect to succeed and he needs to know that someone will be there to explain what the books expect that he was taught long ago. This is not an easy task because there are so many concepts that you expect the child to know that he may not be adequately exposed to during his/her long-term exclusion from the mainstream teaching/learning process. Then, there is the stigma and self-esteem issue that is attached to poor academic performance. In many cases, children are ashamed of not knowing what others think they should know. In trying to hide their lack of knowledge and skill, they may miss out on help that is available for the asking. In the final analysis, parents and concerned individuals have to realize that once a child's academic problems becomes known, it rests on their shoulders to get help for the child and the sooner the better.

One other point that I want to make here is that the son did not begin to test well enough for the mainstream classes overnight. A special education teacher explained that children who are in resource class for learning disabilities are there many times because their test results indicate a significant discrepancy between their ability to learn and their academic performance. In other words, their test result indicate that they have the ability to perform at a higher level. My guess is that this child's potential was there all along, but somewhere along the way he got caught in the shuffle and lingered. In many cases, children recommended into low level classes stay in that tract until they finally get passed out illiterate or drop out of school. As parents, teachers and concerned individuals, we do not want this trend to continue as a plague to our well being.

I have presented only a few case studies where a parent's awareness about their child's educational predicament is crucial in order to ebb the high tide of illiteracy. In the next chapter, let's look at some things that we can do as a start in getting this problem under control.

14
Where Do We Go From Here

There are things that we can do as parents, teachers and individuals who are concerned about the well being of our homes, our communities and our nation.

Parents:
Be Aware of the child's environment

As parents, it is critical to have an awareness of the child's environment. It is important for parents and/or guardians to attend school activities, meetings and conferences even if the child's report card does not indicate a learning problem.

Nurture your child

Nurture and expose your child to many different learning experiences. This can be done by reading, talking, and listening to your child. Take your child for excursions in the park, about the neighborhood, to the library, shopping malls, and other places of interest. The idea is to spend all the time you can with your child. If you are unable to read to your child, find alternative ways to expose your child to reading. Look for programs on the public education television channels that are suitable for your child to learn positive things. Take your child to the library for Children's Story Time and other activities that are available there. Buy books for your child or check some out of the library. This will make your child aware of and ready for learning activities at school and elsewhere. Also, if you expose your child to learning experiences, you will have a good idea what your child knows and will be better able to gauge whether your child needs help in getting ready for school. You will also have an idea when your child is either not being taught at school or is not being taught at the appropriate level.

Maintain open communication with your child

Maintain an open line of communication with your child. Your child should feel free to come to you when there is a problem and not feel that unfair treatment from others is their lot and that they must endure it alone. As parents and guardians of children, we need to know what is going on with our children and the child is a primary source of information in that regard. Talk with your child and talk often. Above all, listen, listen, listen.

Monitor your child's schoolwork

Check the work that your child brings home from school, and make sure it is completed properly. If your child tells you that he does not have any homework, verify this with the teacher. If the child does not have any work, find out why. This can provide a clue for you in the event your child is being excluded from the teaching/learning process. If your child does not bring home individual papers, but brings home a folder every few weeks, you need to be in touch with the teacher because a child can get seriously behind within a few days. The point here is that you need to know how your child is progressing so that you can provide help when needed. If you do not feel adequate to help your child, ask a friend or fellow church member to help you get the help you need for your child.

Where Do We Go From Here

Know your child's potential

Next, you want to know what your child's potential is so that you can do everything in your power to help your child achieve to his potential and challenge his ability to exceed it.

How do you find out what your child's potential is? Children are tested within the school system all the time. Find out from the school counselor what test are given and when. Make a note of this information, and if you do not receive a copy of the results, contact the school for the results, and have it explained to you, if necessary. Check with the school to see how your child is doing in relation to his test scores. If your child is having a problem, find out why, and find out what can be done to correct the problem.

No matter what, when you get the test results, save them so that you can compare them to past and future test results. You want to make sure that your child is not regressing or losing proficiency. Regression can occur when a child is excluded from the teaching/learning process. As a child gets older his test results relate more closely to what he/she is taught in the classroom and other learning situations; the impact of the intelligence quotient diminishes considerably. When you look at your child's test scores, see how it relates to his school work. (Please note that the following suggestion is difficult for many average parents to carry out because it requires knowledge and information that many of us do not have. At the very least, we can ask questions to ascertain how the child is performing in relationship to test scores.) For example, if his test results indicate achievement at grade Level 2.5 in reading, you should know which of the school's reading material is grade Level 2.5. If grade level 2.5 indicates Level 11 and your child is in Level 7; you want to challenge the great disparity and work with the school to see that the discrepancy is effectively addressed. Otherwise, your child will not grow in that area, and unless he receives some outside stimulus, he will begin to lose proficiency.

Another factor to consider when trying to access your child potential is his/her performance on school work and other task. Some children do not test well and other factors should be taken into account when assessments are made. Children should not be excluded from the teaching/learning process simply because they do not test well on standardized test.

Monitor your child's performance

A child is likely to become frustrated and disenchanted with school when he is left out of the teaching/learning process or is not adequately challenged. Also, if the school is allowed to exclude your child from the teaching/learning process, you may see that your child becomes a behavioral problem. Closely following your child's placement early on in the process will help prevent extended periods of performance at levels significantly below potential. An underachiever pattern can develop if your child is not adequately challenged year after year, and eventually he may become disenchanted with school even to the point of dropping out.

Correct situations where your child is not taught

If you discover that the school is not teaching your child at the appropriate levels, take immediate affirmative action to correct the situation. If after you have brought your concerns to the attention of the teacher, and it is not corrected, bring it to the attention of school administrators. If the problem remains unresolved bring it to the attention of the school's community of parents as well. More than likely, your child is not the only one affected. If the situation is brought out into the open, it is more likely that steps will be taken to correct it. A child's future is in the balance, and the child's family and the community will be impacted. Poorly educated children grow up to become burdens on their families, on the communities in which they live, and on society in general.

Remove your child from the bad situation

Most importantly, do not let your child linger in a bad educational environment, one in which their academic needs are not properly addressed. Do not sit idly by and hope for things to get better next month or next year. The likelihood is that things will not get better, as each new year's knowledge is stacked upon the previous year's knowledge. If you feel nervous about the waves you make in an effort to see that your child is taught, look for alternative avenues within the school system and outside, if necessary, until the child's instructional needs are met. But, whatever you do, never allow problems of this serious nature to remain unresolved. Left unresolved, these problems will fester and they can destroy you and your child.

Concerned Individuals and Communities

There are parents who are unable to provide the support needed when their children are excluded from the teaching/learning process or for other reasons have not mastered the basic academic skills. In these situations concerned individuals and groups are needed to fill the void. As concerned individuals, we can do some of the following:

Establish programs to address teaching of basic skills

When children get behind in the primary grades, they need to be taught the basic skills. This is different from tutoring that is task oriented. In task oriented tutoring you work on the task at hand instead of on basic skills in general. Several universities offer programs to address basic and enrichment skills during the Summer. In lieu of setting up a program, concerned individuals can contribute to existing programs to provide fees for students whose parents cannot afford to enroll them.

Tutor children in the basic skills

Volunteer to tutor children in the basis skills or become a part of some of the organizations established to tutor children. If you tutor in schools, make sure you aren't babysitting children who are being removed as a means of excluding them from the teaching/learning process. Make sure that you have material or that you are given material to use as you work with the children.

Establish a task force to provide family literacy support

Because illiteracy has reached such epidemic proportions, we need a task force to provide support for families with children at risk. This task force needs to focus on the identification and correction of problems that cause illiteracy. Details of this task force are beyond the scope of this book. However, The task force should be established at the grassroots level and it should be far reaching in scope. In the early years, we want to know that children are taught the basic skills so they will be able to perform in the classroom and on standardized test. Children should be evaluated before they start school and in Kindergarten, First and Second Grade. They should be monitored to assure that do not lose academic proficiency. At the point they do not perform, children referred to the task force need to be evaluated under the auspices of the task force. The purpose of the evaluation is not the removal of children from the classroom, but to assure that they are taught in the classroom. However, corrective action for skill deficits should be in the plan. An important aspect of the task force is that it should consist of concerned individuals committed to the detection and correction of situations that cause illiteracy in its early stages.

The children referred to here are capable children who become illiterate due to ethnic and racial bias. Many times when we talk about the problem of illiteracy, we bring up parents who do not discipline their children and children who have behavioral problems. However, the children who are the subject of this book, did not necessarily exhibit behavioral problems. But, as many illiterate children grow older, they fear that their options are limited and begin to exhibit deviant behavior. As a result, their positive contribution to society becomes limited. Many will have problems making a living and a life for themselves and those they love. They will be scorned and there are only a few things worse than being down and out, illiterate and scorned.

Teachers
Care About the Children You Teach

Examine yourselves and your attitudes. Remember, when children who are charged to you do not learn, it is a reflection on your unwillingness or inability to teach. Do not let your attitude get in the way of your teaching children. Make sure that you do not find excuses to exclude children from teaching/learning activities. The failure to teach children, regardless of their racial heritage is criminal.
****

**So that was yesterday. It happened in so many yester-
days ago. Yet, each yesterday dawns a tomorrow as today in
the lives of our sons and daughters.**

EPILOGUE

Children become confused and their self-esteem damaged when their academic skills are deficient. Moreover, it is difficult to correct academic deficiencies when a child is continually excluded from the teaching\learning process by design. When a child is not taught in Kindergarten, First Grade and Second Grade, he or she cannot effectively achieve academically in the subsequent grades because the primary skills were not taught and mastered.

When we fail to ensure that all of our children are taught the basic academic skills of reading, writing and arithmetic, we contribute to the problem of illiteracy and ultimately to deviant behavior that is associated with persons who have failed academically in this country.

My hope is that every person who reads this story will take a demonstrative interest in correcting the problems that cause our children to fail. Correcting problems of this nature is the responsibility of entire communities because the problem is bigger than those directly affected. Communities banding together to identify and correct situations which contribute to the failure of our children is imperative. Indeed, it takes a whole village to raise a child.

ESSAY

(Written by Chris somewhere around 8th grade)

A Deadly Disease

Prejudice is a disease that is spreading across our land like a raging bull. Somewhere down the line it must be destroyed before it destroys us. To wipe out racism or prejudice, you must destroy it at the source, which is the mind. Prejudice is a disease that affects the mind. First, the disease pollutes the mind and floods out all logical thoughts. Then it gives you the feeling that you are superior to someone else. If this disease is not driven from the mind, its most harsh affects kick into action. In its most harmful stage, prejudice can cause you to kill and hurt others that you feel are inferior. I must warn you, as dangerous as prejudice is, it is contagious! As I said before, we must destroy prejudice before it destroys us!

Author's Note

In this book, the facts present themselves and are not advanced as indictments against all white teachers and administrators charged with the responsibility of educating minority children. To the contrary, I am convinced that many White teachers properly shoulder their responsibility to teach children regardless of their racial heritage. We continue to expect and need their help as well.

Glossary

Functionally illiterate: Lacking the developmental skills to effectively process letters and numbers in normal day to day activities and interactions.

Teaching /Learning process: The process whereby students learn in a classroom setting as a result of instruction and student/teacher interaction.

Bibliography

Baldwin, James. <u>The Fire Next Time</u>, New York: Vintage International, 1993

Index

School Grades
Preschool:
      Gregory, chapters 1,2,3; Chris, chapters 2,3
Kindergarten:
      Gregory, chapter 2; Chris, chapter 4
First Grade:
      Gregory, chapters 2,3; Chris, chapter 5
Second Grade:
      Gregory, chapter 3; Chris, chapter 6
Third Grade:
      Gregory, chapter 4; Chris, chapter 7
Fourth Grade:
      Gregory, chapter 5; Chris, chapter 7
Fifth Grade:
      Gregory, chapters 6,7; Chris, chapter 8
Junior High:
      Gregory, chapter 7; Chris. chapter 8
High School:
      Gregory, chapter 8; Chris, chapters 8,11
Alternative School:
      Gregory, chapter 9

Documents:

1. Warren Associates test report   pages 67 - 71

2. School District test report   pages 81 - 85

Editor's Note

This is an excellent book. Everyone should read it: parents, educators, and students. Why? This is a very informative and thought provoking book. It asks a lot of questions and it answers a lot of questions. It stirs a lot of emotions. It will make some readers angry and it will make some readers sad. Some will receive revelation, but most important, I believe that many readers will be healed as a result of the reading process.

More Reviews

A NAME I CAN'T READ: The Rocky Road to Literacy, A Mother's Story by Claudia M. Darkins, exposes some real, yet hidden, reasons for illiteracy. Darkins offers African-Americans parents the alarming facts that exist in today's schools, and focuses on how parents who take an active role in their child's education can look forward to positive results. It's a Must Read!

Renee Minus White
THE N.Y. AMSTERDAM NEWS

Only valid documentation convinces one that this is not fiction! Nightmarish were the experiences of the author and her two children! However, as she states, these experiences should not serve as an indictment of all white teachers. I know from personal experience that should not be so because there are black teachers who have been guilty of the same biased treatment of black students and there are white teachers who knock themselves out trying to help black students. Rather the book could serve to alert all educators, parents and communities to the impact they have on young lives and encourage them to be sure that impact is a positive one.

Julius W. Becton Jr.
CEO/Superintendent District of Columbia School System
Former President of Prairie View A&M University

A Name I Can't Read

ORDER FORM

1st Edition - Limited Quantities Available

NAME: _____ _____ _____ **DATE:** _____ **NO.** _____

Last First MI

PRICE: $ **14.95**

QUANTITY × _____

MAIL TO: _____

Address Street

SUBTOTAL _____

TAX : TX 8.25% _____

_____ _____ _____

City State Zip

SHIP/HANDLING _____

PHONE: Day ( ) - Eve ( ) - **TOTAL COST** $ _____

CANE PUBLISHING - P.O. BOX 710544; HOUSTON, TX 77271-0544

PHONE: 713-541-5258 ORDERS: 1-888-599-2263 FAX: 713-541-5256

(PLEASE MAKE CHECK OR MONEY ORDER PAYABLE TO CANE PUBLISHING)

Mail Orders add $4.00 shipping for 1st book & 2.00 for each additional book

Texas residents add 8.25% tax to order subtotal